HOW TO
START A
BUSINESS
IN THE
STATE OF
NEW JERSEY

HOW TO
START A
BUSINESS
IN THE
STATE OF
NEW JERSEY

BY LAWRENCE NOVICK

Retired Professor of Small Business Management & Former Director of
The Small Business Development Center at
Brookdale Community College

ABOUT THE AUTHOR

Lawrence Novick is a retired Management Professor from Brookdale Community College, where he instructed students on the basics of entering their own business. He established the first Small Business Management course and the Small Business Management degree option at the College. Mr. Novick is also the managing partner in an accounting firm that specializes in working with the small business owner.

Professor Novick is the former director of Brookdale's Small Business Development Center where he worked with hundreds of business people, handling any number of business-related problems. The Small Business Administration-sponsored Small Business Institute was also his responsibility, wherein students went out into the business community to assist the business person. Professor Novick has been a guest lecturer throughout the State, speaking to groups on the successful way to start and operate a small business.

This handbook is the result of his many years of teaching the subject of small business, directing government-sponsored assistance programs, and his thirty years as an accountant, working with the small business community.

PREFACE

Over the years many lengthy books have been published discussing the perils of business ownership and how people fail. Several hundred authors have printed texts that suggest how you can replace your accountant and attorney in the early years of a business. There are also a number of excellent small business management publications containing thousands of pages of material far too complicated for the new business owner.

After many years of teaching aspiring business owners and helping my own clients, I have found that there was a great demand for a text such as this one. Why not have one manual that would provide the owner with a simple means to his end wish – that being entering his own business. The materials contained within these pages do just that. The information is designed for the New Jersey business person and it covers such areas as registering your trade name, incorporation materials, working with the New Jersey sales tax bureau, free assistance agencies, and much more information about the State you intend to operate in.

It has always been my feeling that the more informed you appear to your professional the greater respect and attention you will command. Go to their office with more than just an idea; have a basic knowledge of what you intend to accomplish. I am not interested in replacing your accountant or attorney, nor teaching you the finer points of business law, or even preparing you for an intensive tax audit. Rather, I would like to help you enter the business environment just as you might prepare for a new job. Learn as much as you can, be fully aware of the pitfalls, and only then, take the final step.

This current text contains many updates and changes from previous editions. Federal and state agencies now advocate use of their web sites to obtain information, file forms, pay fees or taxes. The most current web addresses are shown. Be aware that these sites and phone numbers continually change.

If you picked up this book, you are seriously considering your own business venture and do not need to be told how to determine if you have the proper personality to be an owner. My plan is encouragement, not discouragement. I am only interested in you being fully prepared for success, not failure.

CONTENTS

1
DETERMINING HOW MUCH MONEY YOU NEED

Before you even think about beginning a new business you must determine how much money will be needed. It is very important to have this information at your fingertips, because one of the major reasons for small business failure is not enough beginning funds.

If you are starting your business out of a home or apartment, the operating expenses will be kept to a minimum. Most of the money you take in will end up as profit, even after paying the costs to keep your business going. By the way, be sure to check with your local town ordinances and zoning laws before you invest large sums of money in renovations or advertising. You might be surprised to discover that one of your neighbors does not want you to be in business next door to him.

When considering a new business (versus an ongoing concern) you have to be a lot more careful in the computation of the dollars necessary to get the new venture started and operating profitably. There are two very important areas which need your close attention. They are:

1. Compute how much money you will need to open up the store or business. In other words, what will it cost you before you do one dollar in sales?

2. The next area of concern is to set up some projection of how many dollars must be generated to break even, and possibly to earn enough money to also pay your personal living expenses.

Let's review and concentrate on the first section: that being the opening costs. Remember, these are probably one-time outlays of dollars that must be paid for during the first months before or shortly after the opening day. Do not simply prepare a list off the "top of your head." Write down the expenditures and obtain the most accurate costs. On the following page is a suggested list of pre-opening costs for almost any new business.

List of Pre-Opening Costs

1. Inventory (stock to sell in the store) $ _____

2. First month's rent   _____

3. Rent security (usually 2 or 3 months)   _____

4. Insurance (paid in advance)   _____

5. Advertising   _____

6. Deposit on utilities   _____

7. Phone installation and required deposit   _____

8. Legal and accounting fees   _____

9. Sales supplies (cards, bags, boxes)   _____

10. Improvements to the shop (decorating/ remodeling   _____

11. Purchase of a van or truck   _____

12. Equipment and fixtures   _____

13. Registering the trade name   _____

14. License and permits   _____

15. Incorporating costs (if you select this form)   _____

16. Alarm system or security gate   _____

17. Sign on the outside   _____

18. Sign on the inside   _____

19. Painting sign on a van or truck   _____

20. Purchase of domain name and web hosting   _____

TOTAL $ _____

Here are some helpful hints relating to the items shown on the pre-opening cost list.

1. **Inventory**

   Most companies will require you to pay for the first order of goods C.O.D. (cash on delivery) or in advance. If any wholesaler will give you time to pay, take advantage of it. This is really an interest-free, short-term loan.

2.3. **Rent**

   This information can be obtained from the landlord when negotiating the lease. Be sure to have your lawyer review your lease before you sign it. There is no such thing as a "standard" lease.

4. **Insurance**

   Obtain the quote from your insurance agent for workmen's compensation, liability, fire, theft, and multi-peril. For additional information call the N.J. Department of Insurance at (609) 292-2516. Be sure to get workers compensation insurance to cover any employees.

5. **Advertising**

   This is a tough area. This amount will vary greatly depending on the media you use. Make sure you get written quotes for your ads.

6.7. **Utilities**

   The electric, gas, and phone companies can provide exact amounts for these categories.

8. **Legal and accounting fees**

   Ask your professional for a realistic estimated cost of services to be rendered.

9. **Sales supplies**

   This section takes in all size bags, business cards, stationery and sales invoices.

10. **Improvements**

   This is another large expenditure, so be careful. This area includes walls (paneling), pegboard, drop ceilings, lights, bathrooms, shelving, cabinets, display fixtures, mirrors, etc. Sometimes the landlord may be willing to do some or all of the improvements in return for an increase in the monthly rent.

11. **Vehicle**

   Purchase only if you need one.

12. **Equipment and fixtures**
   In this area be sure to include cash registers, adding machines, file cabinets, safe, desk, chairs, tables, etc.

13. **Registering trade name**
   Completed at your County Clerk's office – about $55.00.

14. **Licenses and Permits**
   Contact the N.J. State Dept. of Licenses and Permits, Dept. of State, State House, CN 300, Trenton, N.J. 08625-0300 — Attn.: Ombudsman (609) 777-0885. You may also log onto the NJ web site for data:
   https://www.nj.gov/njbusiness/pdfs/liccert.pdf
   This takes you to the NJ web site titled: NJ License & Certification Guide.

15. **Incorporation**
   Let your attorney inform you of the amount of money required here (or you may file on your own).

16-19. **Security systems, signs**
   Get at least three separate quotes for each of these items. Remember, you need a sign big enough for people to see.

20. **Domain name and web site hosting**
   Today even brick and mortar stores need a web presence.

Now that you have figured out how much money you need to start the business, go ahead and count what you have on hand and how much you will be able to borrow. If you cannot come up with the amount necessary to get your business started, give it a hard close second look. Then go back and reevaluate the pre-opening list and costs. Also, don't forget, you may need money in the first six months to carry you through any initial slow period.

2
COMPUTING A
BREAKEVEN TO OPERATE
THE BUSINESS

We are now ready to review the second area, which concerns itself with figuring out a breakeven point. It will be difficult to stay in business if you cannot turn a profit. This part of the book will show you how to set up a budget of income and expenses. Under most conditions the statement of income and expenses starts with receipts (sales, fees, commissions, etc.) on the top and lists all the expenses thereafter. The total expenses are deducted from sales to reach a profit or loss, such as:

AL'S PHOTO SHOP

Month of November

Sale of photos		$1200
Expenses		
Supplies	500	
Phone	45	
Rent	230	
Auto expenses	110	
Total expenses		885

In working out the breakeven, the first step is to set down what you feel will be the costs to operate the business. Let's also make an assumption that your present job pays you $1,000.00 per month gross pay before tax deductions, and that you need to make at least this same amount if you go out on your own.

Here comes the tough part. You must try to estimate the monthly operating costs as accurately as possible. The expenses might include the following items and here we will use estimated amounts to show how to set up the schedule.

	Monthly Estimated Costs
Expenses – Itemized	
Rent	$ 500
Help	400
Utilities	150
Advertising	150
Telephone	80
Delivery Costs	50
Insurance	50
Sales Supplies	40
Water	15
TOTAL	$1435
Total expenses	$1435
Your present earnings	1000
SALES	$2435

This statement shows that you will have to generate net sales or a gross profit of $2,435.00 in order to pay all your expenses and provide a salary to you of $1,000 per month. In income statement form the breakeven computation might appear as follows:

Monthly	$2435
Less Expenses to Operate	1435
Net Profit	$1000

Be careful. If there are any monthly notes or loans to be paid, these should be included in your estimate of expenses for a total monthly cash outlay.

The projected income statement for a retail business is set up a little different. A brief accounting lesson for retail sales: If your selling price is double the cost of your goods, you make a 50% gross profit. To generate $2,435.00 gross profit you must have sales of $4,870.00 and the statement will look like the following (this is also a way to check your computation):

Projected Statement of Income & Expenses			
Sales			$4,870
Cost of sales 50%			—2,435
		Gross Profit	$2,435
Expenses			
Rent	$ 500		
Help	400		
Utilities	150		
Advertising	150		
Telephone	80		
Delivery Costs	50		
Insurance	50		
Sales Supplies	40		
Water	15		
		Total expenses	1,435
		Net Profit	$1,000

Be sure to try and obtain accurate costs. The problem here is that you are estimating sales of $4,870 and if the business cannot generate sales of $4,870, you have a real concern and you should rethink your idea, its worth, and the possibility for success.

3
OBTAINING
THE CAPITAL
TO START

Let's begin to look at where and how you can get the money. Most inexperienced business people immediately think of their bank or some government agency to come up with the bulk of the funds. There are many sources of money for the new business that should be pursued. Once again, before committing yourself to a lease, leaving your full time job or signing a long-term contract, make sure you have your financing in order. The biggest problem of most new owners is that they do not start with enough money in the early years or are incapable of acquiring extra needed dollars later on. Don't get caught up in this trap. Do your planning before you start or – don't start.

The problem here is not whether to borrow, how much interest you should be paying, or how long the payout should be. If you really want to begin your business, where or how you obtain your money or capital will not matter.

Your starting funds may come from one or more of the following sources:

- **Personal funds** – savings account, etc.
- **Personal Bank Loan** – signature or collateral
- **Trade Credit** – here you purchase inventory and pay in 30 to 90 days
- **Loan from a vendor or supplier** – at times vending companies may pay your commissions in advance
- **Friends** – be prepared to pay interest on the loan
- **Small Loan Companies** – very high interest rate
- **Credit Unions**
- **Loans on your Life Insurance** – this is usually very low interest
- **Advance Borrowing through a Credit Card** – very high interest

- Overdraft Checking Account Loans

- Small Business Administration

- Second Mortgage on your home

- Refinancing a first mortgage on your home

- Loans from pension funds

- **Equipment loans or leases** – in these situations the seller of the equipment may allow you to pay for the item over a fixed period of time

- **N. J. Economic Development Authority**

One important factor to consider when you borrow money is to make sure you add the monthly payments into your budget of cash flow along with your expenses.

Another point to incorporate into your business thinking is to *be sure to pay all your notes on time.* Your credit rating with lenders is your most important asset. Without the ability to borrow, you may not be able to expand to other areas, increase your inventory, or even take on more help. Once you neglect to make timely payments on your loans, you effectively cut off your line of credit. When you borrow, do so wisely, and *always* pay your monthly obligation.

A small clue about our banking institutions. At times one gets the feeling they like to lend their money to people who don't need it. When you go to your bank, *look good,* and if they are willing to make a loan, borrow a little more than you need. If you go back a year later when business is slow, you may not be able to get the additional monies.

Before going to any bank to borrow money, find out the bank's policies by contacting lending institutions, and ask the following:

– **Are they lending to borrowers such as yourself**

– **What is the present interest rate – remember the rate may vary with different types of loans**

– **What information will they want to review**

Here is a method that has been used effectively when attempting to get loan approval for a new business. Be prepared and have all your papers in order when you go to the bank.

FOR AN EXISTING OR NEW BUSINESS

- Know exactly how much you need
- Be able to tell the loan officer how the money will help you, such as:
  - increase sales
  - purchase equipment
  - expand your shop
  - hire new employees
  - increase inventory
  - pay for a new advertising program
  - etc.
- Show the officer how these new funds will make you more money
- Have a payment plan in mind (how long before the bank will get its money back)

FOR A NEW BUSINESS

- Describe in detail the type of business to be established
- Be sure to explain your experience and management capabilities related to the business
- Bring along a brief history of yourself and why you are going into this particular business
- Show how much money you or others will invest in the business
- Have with you a current balance sheet listing all personal assets and liabilities
- Prepare a detailed projection of earnings for the first year the business will operate
- If you are incorporated, be aware that the bank may still want you to sign personally on the loan

I enjoy relating a story of how I got my first business loan. A client friend of mine was going to introduce me to his banker from whom I hoped to borrow $5,000 for one year. My preparation for the meeting included a financial history of my firm, a personal resume, why I needed the money, and when I would repay the loan. When I met my friend and discussed the loan, we agreed that a request of $10,000 would no doubt at least get me $5,000. In the elevator going down to the banker I decided to ask for $15,000 and negotiate down to $5,000 or $10,000. After having met the loan officer and having spoken to him for several minutes, I felt more confident and my reply to his question of "How Much?" was

$20,000. Much to my surprise, he said, "OK, how long before you can repay it?" I was delighted in having obtained four times what I needed. I took the $20,000, put $15,000 in a savings account and utilized the $5,000 in the business. After two months I repaid $5,000 on the loan and three months later sent the lender another $7,000. The bank thought I was great. Here I had paid back 60% of the loan in the first five months! In doing so I had earned interest on the extra money borrowed and also saved interest expense by repaying the loan early. My credit record was established and by the end of the twelve months the entire loan was paid off.

4
YOUR BOOKKEEPING SYSTEM

Thus far we have concerned ourselves with determining your financial needs and how to fill them. Now let's proceed to the next step, setting up a bookkeeping system. Once you make the decision to go into your own business, you will be expending funds. The simplest way to keep track of your expenses will be through the use of a checkbook.

If at any time you want to prove that your expenses are business-related and deductible, this is much easier to do if the costs are paid for by a business check. Do not begin paying your bills by cash or even with a small pocket-size checkbook. Also, try not to pay business expenses from your personal checkbook. Remember, attempt to look like a legitimate business concern to all parties concerned about your operation; open a business checking account, and save all your bills.

There are minimum records that must be kept for yourself, the business, and your accountant. Whether you operate by check or cash, you must be able to compute a profit or loss so a tax return can be completed. The outline on page 14 shows the minimum records to maintain for your business.

Here is some sound advice on your record-keeping system and books of original entry.

1. Save all bills and invoices; mark them when paid, noting whether check or cash, and the date paid. After the invoice is paid, be sure to file it where you can locate the bill if needed again.

STATEMENT No. *1612C*

TO *JAMY'S* _____ 20 ____

TERMS:

500 LBS.		#2 FLOUR		₿	25	00
		Paid				
		Ch.# 162				
		5-23-2/				

A PAID INVOICE

RECEIPTS

INCOME

FEES ⎫
COMMISSIONS ⎬ Checks
SALES ⎭
↓
Deposit into Bank
↓
File Deposit Ticket
↓
Record in Ledger

Cash
↓
Deposit into Bank

Cash in
your pocket
↓
Record in Ledger

DISBURSEMENTS

EXPENSES

RENT ⎫
PHONE ⎬ Paid by Cash ⟶ Get a Receipt
ETC. ⎭
↓
Paid by Check
↓
Record on
Check Stub
↓
Note Paid
on Invoice
Save Bill & File
↓
Record in Ledger

Write **PAID** on Bill
Save Bill & File
↓
Record in Ledger

MINIMUM RECORDS TO MAINTAIN

2. Keep a record of all the miles put on your vehicle. Before anything happens, you will have visited an attorney, looked at stores, gone to suppliers and made calls on builders. All these trips are legitimate deductions, even if you are unable to start the business.

NOVEMBER 20____	NOVEMBER 20____
9 MONDAY	THURSDAY **12**
To Red Bank 18 miles Look at store	
10 TUESDAY	FRIDAY **13**
	Went to Rex Lyon Attorney, East Hanover 72 miles
11 WEDNESDAY	SATURDAY **14**
Visit Donut Shoppe Lakewood 36 miles Parking 25¢	bought Journal Cash $5.95 8 miles SUNDAY **15**

DIARY

3. Open and start using a business-type checking account, with your name imprinted on the checks. If you registered the trade name, this should also appear on your checks.

When getting your first business checking account, I would recommend the commercial type setup with a larger size check and checkstub. The best type would be the one that uses a three-ring binder that looks like this.

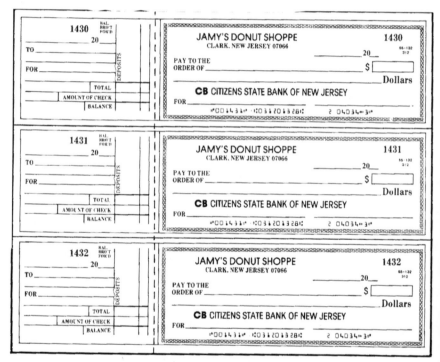

BUSINESS SIZE CHECKS AND
CHECK STUBS

The stub allows enough space to fully explain what is written on the check. The stub can be removed easily from the notebook so that a bookkeeper or accountant can copy information from the stub and into a journal to summarize the checks written. When the task is completed, the stubs can be returned to the notebook and placed back into numerical order.

Many people make the mistake of starting with the small pocket size type. This tiny checkbook is too small to provide adequate information on the check or stub as can be seen from the illustration.

DATE	#	PAYEE	DEBIT	CREDIT	BAL.

JAMY'S DONUT SHOPPE
CLARK, NEW JERSEY 07066

143
55-132
312

_____ 20 ___

PAY TO THE
ORDER OF _____ $ [   ]

_____ Dollars

CB CITIZENS STATE BANK OF NEW JERSEY

FOR _____

⑆00⑈143⑈⑈ ⑉:031⑈20⑈13⑈28⑈: 2 04034⑈3⑈⑈

**POCKET SIZE
CHECKBOOK**

ONE-WRITE SYSTEM

I will explain this system to you, but suggest some caution in starting out with this setup. More than likely, your funds will be limited in the beginning, so you might want to watch your expenditures. A one-write check system could cost you anywhere from $55 to $200 to start. Wait a reasonable length of time to see how business will be, for you can change to this system of bookkeeping at any time.

One of the most important bookkeeping functions is to prepare a summary of all the checks written in your checkbook. The book setup to summarize these checks is called a disbursements journal. When using a regular checking account, your write-up of a check disbursements journal would be completed as follows:

1. You write the check for rent – $375.00

2. Then you enter this information on the stub

3. From the stub you would prepare a check disbursements journal like the one shown below.

DATE	PAYEE	CH. #	AMOUNT	RENT	PURCHASES	PHONE	GEN. ITEMS
5/5	Landlord	106	375.	375.			

CHECK DISBURSEMENTS JOURNAL

When using a one-write type of system, you would only have to do one writing. Actually, the system is rather simple for it uses a carbon strip on the back of the check.

When you write the check, you prepare the check stub and disbursements journal at the same time. This type of bookkeeping system is a great time saver, avoids errors, and is even more effective for payroll record keeping. A typical one-write system for writing checks is shown below.

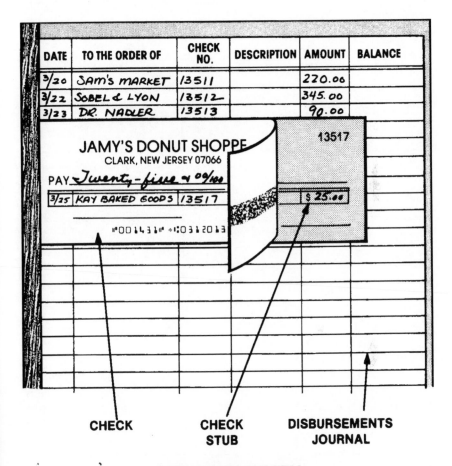

DATE	TO THE ORDER OF	CHECK NO.	DESCRIPTION	AMOUNT	BALANCE
3/20	SAM's MARKET	13511		220.00	
3/22	SOBEL & LYON	13512		345.00	
3/23	DR. NADLER	13513		90.00	
3/25	KAY BAKED GOODS	13517		$ 25.00	

JAMY'S DONUT SHOPPE
CLARK, NEW JERSEY 07066
PAY Twenty-five * 00/100
13517
⑊OO1431⑊ ⑊:031 20 13

CHECK   CHECK STUB   DISBURSEMENTS JOURNAL

ONE-WRITE SYSTEM
DISBURSEMENTS JOURNAL

By using a payroll one-write system you can produce the check, your checkstub, the employee's paystub, payroll journal, and employee's earnings card with one entry. An illustration is shown below.

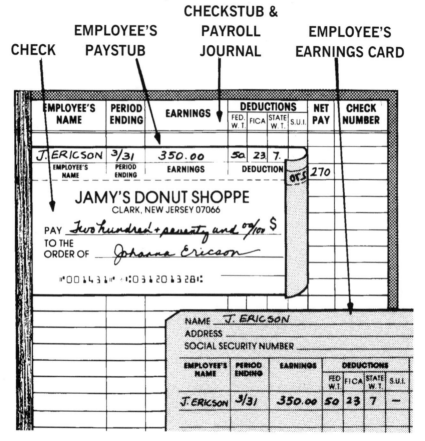

CHECK   **EMPLOYEE'S PAYSTUB**   **CHECKSTUB & PAYROLL JOURNAL**   **EMPLOYEE'S EARNINGS CARD**

ONE-WRITE SYSTEM
PAYROLL JOURNAL

There are many companies that sell these systems of bookkeeping. Have them come speak to you and give you the information and costs for the setup. Many business owners are now utilizing computer-based check writing software to prepare payments, send funds, and maintain bookkeeping records. Before making a final decision, be sure to check with your accountant.

Remember the clearer your records, the easier it will be for your financial advisor to prepare financial statements and do your tax returns.

5
REGISTERING
YOUR
TRADE NAME

When starting a business, many people like to select a name that is different from their own. Often they wish to use a name or phrase that is "catchy" or describes their shop. This name, which is different from their own, is known as a trade name.

The major reason for filing a trade name certificate is to make certain that you can prevent someone else from using your name. You would be very upset if another new business opened in the general area as yours and used the same trade name. After you spend a lot of money advertising Jamy's Donut Shoppe, you do not want to see someone else open up with the same name over the door. Once you file "Jamy's Donut Shoppe," you will have a better chance of preventing other people from using the same trade name in your county.

If you do not incorporate your business, you should help protect your trade name by filing a Trade Name Certificate within the county that you locate your company. The bank will also want to see your approved trade name certificate before allowing you to open a checking account under this fictitious name.

A sample trade name certificate form is shown on the next page for your review. This sheet must be completed, notarized, and then four copies brought to the courthouse in the county you locate the business. The cost will be about $50.00 for the filing.

For informational purposes there are two abbreviations used in trade name presentations.

T/A means "trading as"

and

D.B.A. means "doing business as"

As an example, Jon and Amy Carlin open the donut business and name it Jamy's Donut Shoppe. They may show their name on business checks as:

Jon and Amy Carlin T/A
Jamy's Donut Shoppe

or

Jon and Amy Carlin D.B.A.
Jamy's Donut Shoppe

PLEASE NOTE THAT INFORMATION BECOMES PUBLIC RECORD
CERTIFICATE OF TRADE NAME
Monmouth County, New Jersey
CHRISTINE GIORDANO HANLON, ESQ., MONMOUTH COUNTY CLERK

The undersigned hereby certifies the following:
1. The name under which the undersigned is about to transact business
2. The location where the said business will be conducted
3. The type of business to be conducted by the undersigned
4. The full name(s) and address of each person(s) connected with the said business as owner(s)

The person or persons, partner or partners, member or members of the firm or partnership conducting or transacting the said business, who are not residents in this State, do hereby constitute the Clerk of the County and his/her successors in office wherein this Certificate is filed, the true and lawful attorney of such non-resident person or persons, partner or partners, member or members, upon whom all original process may be served (a) in an action or legal proceeding against said firm or partnership or (b) in an action against said person or persons, partner or partners, member or members, for any debt, damages or liability contracted on incurred by them in, or growing out of, the conduct or transaction of said business in the State of New Jersey. It is agreed that such original process which may be served upon the County Clerk shall be of the same force and validity as if served upon said non-resident person or persons, partner or partners, member or members, of the firm or partnership. The authority hereof shall as to such non-residents, continue in force so long as they shall do, conduct or transact the said business in this State under such name.

TRADE NAME OR DBA _____

CORPORATION NAME _____

ADDRESS 1 _____

ADDRESS 2 _____

CITY/STATE/ZIP _____

PHONE NUMBER (OPTIONAL)_____

DATE REGISTERED _____

DESCRIPTION OF BUSINESS _____

OWNER #1 NAME _____

STREET ADDRESS _____

CITY/STATE/ZIP _____

SIGNATURE _____

OWNER #2 NAME _____

STREET ADDRESS _____

CITY/STATE/ZIP _____

SIGNATURE _____

OWNER #3 NAME _____

STREET ADDRESS _____

CITY/STATE/ZIP _____

SIGNATURE _____

State of New Jersey
County of Monmouth

Sworn and subscribed to before me this _____ day of _____, 20____

_____
Notary Public

County Court Houses in the State of New Jersey are noted on the following pages. Be sure to call the county clerk before bringing your form there. On the next page is a copy of the instruction sheet given to trade name applicants in Monmouth County.

LOCATIONS OF THE
NEW JERSEY COUNTY CLERKS

ATLANTIC COUNTY
County Clerk: Edward McGettigan
5901 Main Street, Box 2005
Mays Landing, NJ 08330
(609) 641-7867
Record Room: (609) 625-4011
Fax: (609) 909-5107

BERGEN COUNTY
County Clerk: John Hogan
One Bergen Plaza, Room 130
Hackensack, NJ 07601-7000
(201) 336-7006
Fax (201) 336-7002
Registry Division, Room 214
(201) 646-2082

BURLINGTON COUNTY
County Clerk: Timothy Tyler
Court Complex, ROOm 104
49 Rancocas Road
Mount Holly, NJ 08060
(609) 265-5122
Fax: (609) 265-0696

CAMDEN COUNTY
County Clerk: Joseph Ripa
100 University Court, 1st Floor
Blackwood, NJ 08012
(865) 225-7219
Fax (856)-756-2213

CAPE MAY COUNTY
County Clerk: Rita Marie Fulginiti
7 N. Main St., PO Box 5000
Cape May, NJ 08210-5000
(609) 465-1013
Fax: (609) 465-8625

CUMBERLAND COUNTY
County Clerk: Celeste Riley
Court House Bldg.
60 West Broad St.
Bridgeton, NJ 08302
(856) 453-4860
Fax: (856) 455-1410

ESSEX COUNTY
County Clerk: Chistopher Durkin
465 Dr. Martin Luther King Jr.Blvd.
Newark, NJ 07102
(973) 621-4921
Fax: (973) 621-2527/2537

GLOUCESTER COUNTY
County Clerk: James N. Hogan
Court House, 1st Floor
1 N. Broad St., PO Box 129
Woodbury, NJ 08096-3327
(856) 853-3241
Fax: (856) 853-3327

HUDSON COUNTY
County Clerk: Barbara A. Netchert
Hudson County Plaza
257 Cornelison Ave. 4th Floor
Jersey City, NJ 07302
(201) 369-7740
Fax: (201) 369-7743

HUNTERDON COUNTY
County Clerk: Mary H. Melfi
Hall of Records
71 Main Street
Flemington, NJ 08822
(908) 788-1214
Fax: (908)782-4068

OFFICE OF THE COUNTY CLERK
COUNTY OF MONMOUTH

CHRISTINE GIORDANO HANLON, ESQ.
COUNTY CLERK

OFFICE OF THE COUNTY CLERK
MARKET YARD, P.O. BOX 1251
FREEHOLD, NJ 07728-1251
732-431-7324

PROCEDURE FOR FILING A TRADE NAME
IN MONMOUTH COUNTY

IT IS THE BUSINESS OWNER'S RESPONSIBILITY TO VERIFY THAT THE TRADE NAME CHOSEN IS NOT CURRENTLY IN USE EITHER IN THIS COUNTY OR IN THE STATE OF NEW JERSEY AS A CORPORATION.

1. Search the records in the Deed Room of the County Clerk's Office in Freehold for the availability of the name you wish to file. This will require searching in the computer and in the books.

2. Be aware that filing a trade name is only effective in the county in which it is filed. It is possible that the business name exists in another county or as a corporation in the State of New Jersey.

3. The Certificate of Trade Name must be filled out and notarized in our office. **DO NOT SIGN THE FORM UNTIL YOU ARE IN THE RECORDING OFFICE**. The following will be required:

   a. Identification (driver's license, passport, etc.)
   b. $54.00 – cash, money order, master card or visa
   c. All parties involved must be present
   d. Filing fees are non-refundable

4. You will receive two recorded copies of the trade name, one of which your bank may require to open a business account. We will keep the original, and send a copy to the Secretary of State.

5. You must also register your business with the State of New Jersey, Division of Taxation in Trenton (New Business Guide and Information provided when you bring the Trade Name Form in for recording).

MONMOUTH COUNTY CHECKLIST FOR
REGISTERING A TRADE NAME

MERCER COUNTY

County Clerk: Paula Sollami-Covello
240 W. State Street, 7th Floor
PO Box 8068
Trenton, NJ 08650-0068
(609) 989-6494
Fax: (609) 989-1111

MIDDLESEX COUNTY

County Clerk: Elaine Flynn
75 Bayard Street, 4th Floor
PO Box 1110
New Brunswick, NJ 08901-1110
(732) 745-4202
Fax: (732) 745-2170

MONMOUTH COUNTY

County Clerk: Giordano Hanlon
300 Halls Mill Road
Freehold, NJ 07728-1254
(732) 431-7790
Fax: (732) 431-7870

MORRIS COUNTY

County Clerk: Ann Grossi
Administrative & Records Bldg.
PO Box 315 - 10 Court Street
Morristown, NJ 07963-0315
(973) 285-6066
Fax: (973) 285-5233

OCEAN COUNTY

County Clerk: Scott Colabella
PO Box 2191
Toms River, NJ 08754
(732) 929-2110
Fax: (732) 349-4336

PASSAIC COUNTY

County Clerk: Kristen Corrado
401 Grand St., Room 130
Paterson, NJ 07505
(973) 225-3632
Fax: (973) 754-1920

SALEM COUNTY

County Clerk: Kriston Corrado
92 Market Street, PO Box 18
Salem, NJ 08079
(856) 935-7510, Ext. 8208
Fax: (856) 935-8882

SOMERSET COUNTY

County Clerk: Brett Radi
Adm. Bldg., Room 110
PO Box 3000, 20 Grove Street
Somerville, NJ 08876-1262
(908) 231-7006
Fax: (908) 253-8853

SUSSEX COUNTY

County Clerk: Jeff Parrott
Hall of Records Bldg.
83 Spring Street, Ste 304
Newton, NJ 07860-1795
(973) 579-0900
Fax: (973) 383-7493

UNION COUNTY

County Clerk: Joanne Rajoppi
2 Broad St., Room 113
Elizabeth, NJ 07207
(908) 527-4787
Fax: (908) 558-2589

WARREN COUNTY

County Clerk: Patricia Kolb
413 2nd Street
Belvidere, NJ 07823-1500
(908) 475-6211
Fax: (908) 475-6208

6
OBTAINING A FEDERAL EMPLOYMENT NUMBER AND REGISTERING WITH THE STATE OF NEW JERSEY

When you go to the bank to start a business checking account, they will require a federal identification number. This particular number is obtained through application to the Internal Revenue Service on Form SS4. The nine-digit number that will be assigned to your company is like a social security number for a business.

Regardless of the type of ownership you select, the bank will want to see your identification number. If you choose the partnership or corporate organization in which to operate, the federal government requires that you have a federal identification number.

The federal SS4 form is usually one of the major papers completed by your accountant when he "sets up your books." The application is relatively simple to complete and can be done by following the step-by-step directions on the form. The completed form is shown on page 27 and once completed is mailed to the I.R.S.at EIN Operation, Cincinnati, OH 45999. You may also apply by phone at 800-829-4933 or fax the completed application to 855-641-6935. Applications can also be completed online by going to the web site: www.IRS.GOV/Business. Remember, this is a federal form and has nothing to do with the State of New Jersey.

Refer to pages 28, 29 and 30 for specific information relating to the applicaion in regards to applying by telephone, by fax, or online. This material has been printed directly from the IRS web site.

Application for Employer Identification Number

(For use by employers, corporations, partnerships, trusts, estates, churches, government agencies, Indian tribal entities, certain individuals, and others.)

► See separate instructions for each line. ► Keep a copy for your records.

OMB No. 1545-0003

EIN

Type or print clearly.	**1** Legal name of entity (or individual) for whom the EIN is being requested **THE CARLIN PARTNERSHIP**	
	2 Trade name of business (if different from name on line 1) **JAMY'S DONUT SHOPPE**	**3** Executor, administrator, trustee, "care of" name
	4a Mailing address (room, apt., suite no. and street, or P.O. box) **44 DONNA COURT**	**5a** Street address (if different) (Do not enter a P.O. box.)
	4b City, state, and ZIP code (if foreign, see instructions) **CLARK, NEW JERSEY 07066**	**5b** City, state, and ZIP code (if foreign, see instructions)
	6 County and state where principal business is located **UNION, NEW JERSEY**	
	7a Name of responsible party **AMY CARLIN**	**7b** SSN, ITIN, or EIN **123-45-6789**

8a Is this application for a limited liability company (LLC) (or a foreign equivalent)? . . . . ☐ Yes ☑ No   **8b** If 8a is "Yes," enter the number of LLC members . . . . ►

8c If 8a is "Yes," was the LLC organized in the United States? . . . . ☐ Yes ☐ No

9a Type of entity (check only one box). **Caution.** If 8a is "Yes," see the instructions for the correct box to check.

☐ Sole proprietor (SSN) _____
☑ Partnership
☐ Corporation (enter form number to be filed) ► _____
☐ Personal service corporation
☐ Church or church-controlled organization
☐ Other nonprofit organization (specify) ► _____
☐ Other (specify) ►

☐ Estate (SSN of decedent) _____
☐ Plan administrator (TIN) _____
☐ Trust (TIN of grantor) _____
☐ National Guard ☐ State/local government
☐ Farmers' cooperative ☐ Federal government/military
☐ REMIC ☐ Indian tribal governments/enterprises
Group Exemption Number (GEN) if any ►

9b If a corporation, name the state or foreign country (if applicable) where incorporated

State | Foreign country

10 Reason for applying (check only one box)
☑ Started new business (specify type) ► _____
BAKERY
☐ Hired employees (Check the box and see line 13.)
☐ Compliance with IRS withholding regulations
☐ Other (specify) ►

☐ Banking purpose (specify purpose) ► _____
☐ Changed type of organization (specify new type) ► _____
☐ Purchased going business
☐ Created a trust (specify type) ► _____
☐ Created a pension plan (specify type) ► _____

11 Date business started or acquired (month, day, year). See instructions.
JANUARY 1, 2017

12 Closing month of accounting year   **DECEMBER**

13 Highest number of employees expected in the next 12 months (enter -0- if none). If no employees expected, skip line 14.

14 If you expect your employment tax liability to be $1,000 or less in a full calendar year **and** want to file Form 944 annually instead of Forms 941 quarterly, check here. (Your employment tax liability generally will be $1,000 or less if you expect to pay $4,000 or less in total wages.) If you do not check this box, you must file Form 941 for every quarter. ☐

Agricultural	Household	Other
		6

15 First date wages or annuities were paid (month, day, year). **Note.** If applicant is a withholding agent, enter date income will first be paid to nonresident alien (month, day, year) . . . . ►   **JANUARY 8, 2017**

16 Check **one** box that best describes the principal activity of your business.
☐ Construction ☐ Rental & leasing ☐ Transportation & warehousing ☐ Health care & social assistance ☐ Wholesale-agent/broker
☐ Real estate ☐ Manufacturing ☐ Finance & insurance ☐ Accommodation & food service ☐ Wholesale-other ☑ Retail
☐ Other (specify)

17 Indicate principal line of merchandise sold, specific construction work done, products produced, or services provided.
BAKERY PRODUCTS

18 Has the applicant entity shown on line 1 ever applied for and received an EIN? ☐ Yes ☑ No
If "Yes," write previous EIN here ►

	Complete this section **only** if you want to authorize the named individual to receive the entity's EIN and answer questions about the completion of this form.		
Third Party Designee	Designee's name		Designee's telephone number (include area code) ( )
	Address and ZIP code		Designee's fax number (include area code) ( )

Under penalties of perjury, I declare that I have examined this application, and to the best of my knowledge and belief, it is true, correct, and complete.

Name and title (type or print clearly) ► **AMY CARLIN**

Applicant's telephone number (include area code)
(**732**) **555-2738**

Signature ►   Date ►

Applicant's fax number (include area code)
(**732**) **555-2739**

For Privacy Act and Paperwork Reduction Act Notice, see separate instructions.   Cat. No. 16055N   Form **SS-4** (Rev. 1-2010)

APPLICATION FOR
EMPLOYER IDENTIFICATION NUMBER

Instructions for Form SS-4
(Rev. February 2016)

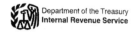

**Department of the Treasury
Internal Revenue Service**

**Application for Employer Identification Number (EIN)
Use with Form SS-4 (Rev. January 2010)**

Section references are to the Internal Revenue Code unless otherwise noted.

General Instructions

Use these instructions to complete Form SS-4, Application for Employer Identification Number (EIN). Also see *Do I Need an EIN?* on page 2 of Form SS-4.

Future Developments

For the latest information related to Form SS-4 and its instructions, such as legislation enacted after they were published, go to *www.irs.gov/ss4.*

Purpose of Form

Use Form SS-4 to apply for an EIN. An EIN is a nine-digit number (for example, 12-3456789) assigned to sole proprietors, corporations, partnerships, estates, trusts, and other entities for tax filing and reporting purposes. The information you provide on this form will establish your business tax account.

 See Form SS-4PR (for Puerto Rico) for the Spanish-language version of Form SS-4.

 An EIN is for use in connection with your business activities only. Don't use your EIN in place of your social security number (SSN) or individual taxpayer identification number (ITIN).

Reminders

Apply for an EIN online. For applicants in the U.S. or U.S. possessions, you can apply for and receive an EIN free of charge on IRS.gov. See *How To Apply for an EIN,* later.

File only one Form SS-4. Generally, a sole proprietor should file only one Form SS-4 and needs only one EIN, regardless of the number of businesses operated as a sole proprietorship or trade names under which a business operates. However, if a sole proprietorship incorporates or enters into a partnership, a new EIN is required. Also, each corporation in an affiliated group must have its own EIN.

 For information about EINs and federal tax deposits, see Pub. 15, Pub. 51 and Pub. 80.

 To ensure fair and equitable treatment for all taxpayers, EIN issuances are limited to one per responsible party, per day. For trusts, the limitation is applied to the grantor, owner, or trustor. For estates, the limitation is applied to the decedent (decedent estate) or the debtor (bankruptcy estate). This limitation is applicable to all requests for EINs whether online, telephone, fax, or mail.

How To Apply for an EIN

You can apply for an EIN online (only for applicants in the U.S. or U.S. possessions), by telephone (only for applicants outside of the U.S. or U.S. possessions), by fax, or by mail, depending on how soon you need to use the EIN. Use only one method for each entity so you don't receive more than one EIN for an entity.

Apply for an EIN online. If you have a legal residence, principal place of business, or principal office or agency in the U.S. or U.S. possessions, you can receive an EIN online and use

it immediately to file a return or make a payment. Go to the IRS website at *www.irs.gov/businesses* and click on *Employer ID Numbers.*

The principal officer, general partner, grantor, owner, trustor, etc. must have a valid Taxpayer Identification Number (SSN, EIN, or ITIN) in order to use the online application. Taxpayers who apply online have an option to view, print, and save their EIN assignment notice at the end of the session. (Authorized third party designees will receive the EIN; however, the EIN assignment notice will be mailed to the applicant.)

 If you have NO legal residence, principal place of business, or principal office or agency in the U.S. or U.S. possessions, you can't use the online application to obtain an EIN. Please use one of the other methods to apply.

Apply by telephone—option available to international applicants only. If you have NO legal residence, principal place of business, or principal office or agency in the U.S. or U.S. possessions, you may call 267-941-1099 (not a toll-free number), 6:00 a.m. to 11:00 p.m. (Eastern time), Monday through Friday, to obtain an EIN.

The person making the call must be authorized to receive the EIN and answer questions concerning Form SS-4. Complete the Third Party Designee section only if you want to authorize the named individual to receive the entity's EIN and answer questions about the completion of Form SS-4. The designee's authority terminates at the time the EIN is assigned and released to the designee. You must complete the signature area for the authorization to be valid.

Note. It will be helpful to complete Form SS-4 before contacting the IRS. An IRS representative will use the information from Form SS-4 to establish your account and assign you an EIN. Write the number you're given on the upper right corner of the form and sign and date it. Keep this copy for your records.

If requested by an IRS representative, mail or fax the signed Form SS-4 (including any third party designee authorization) within 24 hours to the IRS address provided by the IRS representative.

 IRS no longer issues EINs by telephone for domestic taxpayers. Only international applicants can receive an EIN by telephone.

Apply by fax. Under the Fax-TIN program, you can receive your EIN by fax generally within 4 business days. Complete and fax Form SS-4 to the IRS using the appropriate fax number listed in *Where To File or Fax,* later. A long-distance charge to callers outside of the local calling area will apply. Fax-TIN numbers can only be used to apply for an EIN. The numbers may change without notice. Fax-TIN is available 24 hours a day, 7 days a week.

Be sure to provide your fax number so the IRS can fax the EIN back to you.

Apply by mail. Complete Form SS-4 at least 4 to 5 weeks before you will need an EIN. Sign and date the application and mail it to the appropriate address listed in *Where To File or Fax,* later. You will receive your EIN in the mail in approximately 4 weeks. Also see *Third Party Designee,* later.

Call 1-800-829-4933 to verify a number or to ask about the status of an application by mail.

Mar 16, 2016

Cat. No. 62736F

INSTRUCTIONS FOR APPLICATION FOR EMPLOYER IDENTIFICATION NUMBER

Form SS-4 downloaded from IRS.gov is a fillable form and, when completed, is suitable for faxing or mailing to the IRS.

Where To File or Fax

If you have a principal place of business, office or agency, or legal residence in the case of an individual, located in:	File or Fax to:
One of the 50 states or the District of Columbia	Internal Revenue Service Attn: EIN Operation Cincinnati, OH 45999 Fax: (859) 669-5760
If you have no legal residence, principal office or principal agency in any state or the District of Columbia (international/U.S. possessions)	Internal Revenue Service Attn: EIN International Operation Cincinnati, OH 45999 Fax: (859) 669-5987

How To Get Tax Help, Forms, and Publications

 Tax help for your business is available at www.irs.gov/ businesses.

You can download or print all of the forms and publications you may need on www.irs.gov/formspubs. Otherwise, you can go to www.irs.gov/orderforms to place an order and have forms mailed to you. You should receive your order within 10 business days.

Related Forms and Publications

The following forms and instructions may be useful to filers of Form SS-4.
• Form 11-C, Occupational Tax and Registration Return for Wagering.
• Form 637, Application for Registration (For Certain Excise Tax Activities).
• Form 720, Quarterly Federal Excise Tax Return.
• Form 730, Monthly Tax Return for Wagers.
• Form 941, Employer's QUARTERLY Federal Tax Return.
• Form 944, Employer's ANNUAL Federal Tax Return.
• Form 990-T, Exempt Organization Business Income Tax Return.
• Instructions for Form 990-T.
• Form 1023, Application for Recognition of Exemption Under Section 501(c)(3) of the Internal Revenue Code.
• Form 1024, Application for Recognition of Exemption Under Section 501(a).
• Schedule C (Form 1040), Profit or Loss From Business (Sole Proprietorship).
• Schedule F (Form 1040), Profit or Loss From Farming.
• Instructions for Form 1041 and Schedules A, B, G, J, and K-1, U.S. Income Tax Return for Estates and Trusts.
• Form 1042, Annual Withholding Tax Return for U.S. Source Income of Foreign Persons.
• Form 1042-S, Foreign Person's U.S. Source Income Subject to Withholding.
• Instructions for Form 1065, U.S. Return of Partnership Income.
• Instructions for Form 1066, U.S. Real Estate Mortgage Investment Conduit (REMIC) Income Tax Return.
• Instructions for Form 1120, U.S. Corporation Income Tax Return.
• Form 1120S, U.S. Income Tax Return for an S Corporation.
• Form 2290, Heavy Highway Vehicle Use Tax Return.
• Form 2553, Election by a Small Business Corporation.

• Form 2848, Power of Attorney and Declaration of Representative.
• Form 8821, Tax Information Authorization.
• Form 8822-B, Change of Address or Responsible Party — Business.
• Form 8832, Entity Classification Election.
• Form 8849, Claim for Refund of Excise Taxes.

For more information about filing Form SS-4 and related issues, see:
• Pub. 15, Employer's Tax Guide.
• Pub. 51, Agricultural Employer's Tax Guide.
• Pub. 80, Federal Tax Guide for Employers in the U.S. Virgin Islands, Guam, American Samoa, and the Commonwealth of the Northern Mariana Islands.
• Pub. 538, Accounting Periods and Methods.
• Pub. 542, Corporations.
• Pub. 557, Tax-Exempt Status for Your Organization.
• Pub. 583, Starting a Business and Keeping Records.
• Pub. 966, Electronic Choices to Pay All Your Federal Taxes.
• Pub. 1635, Understanding Your EIN.

Specific Instructions

Follow the instructions for each line to expedite processing and to avoid unnecessary IRS requests for additional information. Enter "N/A" on the lines that don't apply.

Line 1. Legal name of entity (or individual) for whom the EIN is being requested. Enter the legal name of the entity (or individual) applying for the EIN exactly as it appears on the social security card, charter, or other applicable legal document. An entry is required.

Individuals. Enter your first name, middle initial, and last name. If you're a sole proprietor, enter your individual name, not your business name. Enter your business name on line 2. Don't use abbreviations or nicknames on line 1.

Trusts. Enter the name of the trust as it appears on the trust instrument.

Estate of a decedent. Enter the name of the estate. For an estate that has no legal name, enter the name of the decedent followed by "Estate."

Partnerships. Enter the legal name of the partnership as it appears in the partnership agreement.

Corporations. Enter the corporate name as it appears in the corporate charter or other legal document creating it.

Plan administrators. Enter the name of the plan administrator. A plan administrator who already has an EIN should use that number.

Line 2. Trade name of business. Enter the trade name of the business if different from the legal name. The trade name is the "doing business as" (DBA) name.

⚠ *Use the full name shown on line 1 on all tax returns filed for the entity. (However, if you enter a trade name on line 2 and choose to use the trade name instead of the legal name, enter the trade name on all returns you file.) To prevent processing delays and errors, use only the legal name (or the trade name) on all tax returns.*

Line 3. Executor, administrator, trustee, "care of" name. For trusts, enter the name of the trustee. For estates, enter the name of the executor, administrator, or other fiduciary. If the entity applying has a designated person to receive tax information, enter that person's name as the "care of" person. Enter the individual's first name, middle initial, and last name.

Lines 4a–b. Mailing address. Enter the mailing address for the entity's correspondence. If the entity's address is outside the United States or its possessions, you must enter the city, province or state, postal code, and the name of the country. Don't abbreviate the country name. If line 3 is completed, enter

-2-   Instr. for Form SS-4 (Rev. 2-2016)

INSTRUCTIONS (CONTINUED) FOR
APPLICATION FOR
EMPLOYER
IDENTIFICATION NUMBER

the address for the executor, trustee, or "care of" person. Generally, this address will be used on all tax returns.

If the entity is filing the Form SS-4 only to obtain an EIN for the Form 8832, use the same address where you would like to have the acceptance or nonacceptance letter sent.

 File Form 8822-B to report any subsequent changes to the entity's mailing address.

Lines 5a–b. Street address. Provide the entity's physical address only if different from its mailing address shown in lines 4a–b. Don't enter a P.O. box number here. If the entity's address is outside the United States or its possessions, you must enter the city, province or state, postal code, and the name of the country. Don't abbreviate the country name.

Line 6. County and state where principal business is located. Enter the entity's primary physical location.

Lines 7a–b. Name of responsible party. Enter the full name (first name, middle initial, last name, if applicable) and SSN, ITIN, or EIN of the entity's responsible party, as defined later.

Responsible party defined. For entities with shares or interests traded on a public exchange, or which are registered with the Securities and Exchange Commission, "responsible party" is (a) the principal officer, if the business is a corporation; (b) a general partner, if a partnership; (c) the owner of an entity that is disregarded as separate from its owner (disregarded entities owned by a corporation enter the corporation's name and EIN); or (d) a grantor, owner, or trustor, if a trust. For tax-exempt organizations, the "responsible party" is commonly the same as the "principal officer" as defined in the Form 990 instructions. For government entities, the "responsible party" is generally the individual in a position to legally bind the particular government entity.

For all other entities, "responsible party" is the individual who has a level of control over, or entitlement to, the funds or assets in the entity that, as a practical matter, enables the individual, directly or indirectly, to control, manage, or direct the entity and the disposition of its funds and assets. The ability to fund the entity or the entitlement to the property of the entity alone, however, without any corresponding authority to control, manage, or direct the entity (such as in the case of a minor child beneficiary), doesn't cause the individual to be a responsible party.

 File Form 8822-B to report any subsequent changes to responsible party information.

If the responsible party is an alien individual with a previously assigned ITIN, enter the ITIN in the space provided and submit a copy of an official identifying document. If necessary, complete Form W-7, Application for IRS Individual Taxpayer Identification Number, to obtain an ITIN.

You must enter an SSN, ITIN, or EIN on line 7b unless the only reason you're applying for an EIN is to make an entity classification election (see Regulations sections 301.7701-1 through 301.7701-3) and you're a nonresident alien or other foreign entity with no effectively connected income from sources within the United States.

Lines 8a–c. Limited liability company (LLC) information. An LLC is an entity organized under the laws of a state or foreign country as a limited liability company. For federal tax purposes, an LLC may be treated as a partnership or corporation or be disregarded as an entity separate from its owner.

By default, a domestic LLC with only one member is disregarded as an entity separate from its owner and must include all of its income and expenses on the owner's tax return (for example, Schedule C (Form 1040)). For more information on single-member LLCs, see *Disregarded entities*, later.

Also by default, a domestic LLC with two or more members is treated as a partnership. A domestic LLC may file Form 8832 to avoid either default classification and elect to be classified as an association taxable as a corporation. For more information on entity classifications (including the rules for foreign entities), see Form 8832 and its instructions.

If the answer to line 8a is "Yes," enter the number of LLC members. If the LLC is owned solely by an individual and his or her spouse in a community property state and they choose to treat the entity as a disregarded entity, enter "1" on line 8b.

 Don't file Form 8832 if the LLC accepts the default classifications above. If the LLC timely files Form 2553, it will be treated as a corporation as of the effective date of the S corporation election as long as it meets all other requirements to qualify as an S corporation. The LLC doesn't need to file Form 8832 in addition to Form 2553. See the Instructions for Form 2553.

Line 9a. Type of entity. Check the box that best describes the type of entity applying for the EIN. If you're an alien individual with an ITIN previously assigned to you, enter the ITIN in place of a requested SSN.

 This isn't an election for a tax classification of an entity. See Disregarded entities, *later.*

Sole proprietor. Check this box if you file Schedule C, or Schedule F (Form 1040) and have a qualified plan, or are required to file excise, employment, alcohol, tobacco, or firearms returns, or are a payer of gambling winnings. Enter your SSN or ITIN in the space provided. If you're a nonresident alien with no effectively connected income from sources within the United States, you don't need to enter an SSN or ITIN.

Corporation. This box is for any corporation other than a personal service corporation. If you check this box, enter the income tax form number to be filed by the entity in the space provided.

 If you entered "1120S" after the Corporation checkbox, the corporation must file Form 2553 no later than the 15th day of the 3rd month of the tax year the election to become an S corporation is to take effect. Until Form 2553 has been received and approved, you will be considered a Form 1120 filer. See the Instructions for Form 2553.

Personal service corporation. Check this box if the entity is a personal service corporation. An entity is a personal service corporation for a tax year only if:
• The principal activity of the entity during the testing period (generally the prior tax year) for the tax year is the performance of personal services substantially by employee-owners, and
• The employee-owners own at least 10% of the fair market value of the outstanding stock in the entity on the last day of the testing period.

Personal services include performance of services in such fields as accounting, actuarial science, architecture, consulting, engineering, health (including veterinary services), law, and the performing arts. For more information about personal service corporations, see the Instructions for Form 1120 and Pub. 542.

 If the corporation is recently formed, the testing period begins on the first day of its tax year and ends on the earlier of the last day of its tax year, or the last day of the calendar year in which its tax year begins.

Other nonprofit organization. Check the *Other nonprofit organization* box if the nonprofit organization is other than a church or church-controlled organization and specify the type of nonprofit organization (for example, an educational organization).

 If the organization also seeks tax-exempt status, you must file either Form 1023 (or Form 1023-EZ) or Form 1024. See Pub. 557 for more information.

Instr. for Form SS-4 (Rev. 2-2016)   -3-

INSTRUCTIONS (CONTINUED) FOR APPLICATION FOR EMPLOYER IDENTIFICATION NUMBER

COMPLETING THE STATE OF NEW JERSEY FORM NJ REG
(Application for Business Registration and Sales Tax)

This particular application is similar to the SS4 form because it alerts the State of New Jersey to the fact that you are in business. The information requested is basically the same as the federal form, but goes one step further. The rear of this form alerts the State to the fact that you will be responsible for sales tax. The form should be filed by all new businesses including sole proprietorships, partnerships and corporations.

The front of the registration form with letters A—N are questions of a general nature about the business and its owner(s). Letters I and J require that you refer to the State's instruction form to fill in the proper codes.

The back of this form asks questions about sales tax, employees and various license requirements. Be sure to answer all the questions since the State will forward to you the sales filing data and employee withholding tables.

The addresses of the New Jersey Sales Tax Offices are noted on page 43. If you place a call to any of these locations, they will gladly mail you the necessary applications or you may write to the:

Division of Taxation
Information Section
CN 999
Trenton, New Jersey 08625

For registration information, the phone numbers are:

(609) 292-9292, (800) 323-4400, fax (609) 984-6851.

To register online, the state web site is:

www.nj.gov/njbusiness/starting/

STATE OF NEW JERSEY
DIVISION OF REVENUE
BUSINESS REGISTRATION APPLICATION
Please read instructions carefully before filling out this form
ALL SECTIONS MUST BE FULLY COMPLETED

* NO FEE REQUIRED *

MAIL TO:
CLIENT REGISTRATION
PO BOX 252
TRENTON, NJ 08646-0252

OVERNIGHT DELIVERY:
CLIENT REGISTRATION
33 West State St 3rd FL
TRENTON, NJ 08608

Hotline
(609) 292-9292
www.nj.gov/treasury/revenue/

REGISTRATION DETAIL

A. Please indicate the reason for your filing this application:
☐ 1. Original application for a new business
☒ Moved previously registered business to new location (REG-C-L can be used in lieu of NJ-REG)
☒ Amended application for an existing business *STARTING PAYROLL*
Reason(s) for amending application: _____
☐ Application for an additional location of an existing registered business
☐ Applying for a Business Registration Certificate   ☐ Employer of Domestic Household Employee(s)
☐ Withholding for Employee(s) residing in NJ (Not doing business or employing in NJ)

B. FEIN # `2` `2` `2` `2` `2` `2` `2` `2` `2`   OR Soc. Sec. # of Owner `☐☐☐` `☐☐` `☐☐☐☐`
☐ Check Box if "Applied for"

C. Name *JON AND AMY CARLIN*
(If your business entity is a Corporation, LLC, LLP, LP or Non-Profit Organization, give entity name. IF NOT, give Name of Owner or Partners)

D. Trade Name *JAMY'S DONUT SHOPPE*

E. Business Location: (Do not use P.O. Box for Location Address)
Street *44 DONNA COURT*
City *CLARK*   State *NJ*
Zip Code `0` `7` `0` `6` `6` `1` `2` `3` `4`
(Give 9-digit Zip)
(See instructions for providing alternate addresses)

F. Mailing Name and Address: (if different from business address)
Name _____
Street _____
City _____   State _____
Zip Code `☐☐☐☐☐`
(Give 9-digit Zip)

BUSINESS DETAIL

G. Beginning date for this business: `1` / `1` / `17` (see instructions)
month / day / year
O/C ___

H. Type of ownership (check one):
☐ NJ Corporation   ☐ Sole Proprietor   ☒ Partnership   ☐ Out-of-State Corporation   ☐ LLP   ☐ Other_____
☐ Limited Partnership   ☐ LLC (1065 Filer)   ☐ LLC (1120 Filer)   ☐ LLC (Single Member)   ☐ S Corporation (You must complete page 41)

I. New Jersey Business Code `5` `3` `0` `6` (see instructions) ☐ Domestic (Household Employer)

J. County / Municipality Code `2` `0` `0` `7` (see instructions) K. County *UNION*
(New Jersey only)

FOR OFFICIAL USE ONLY
DLN _____

L. Will this business be SEASONAL? ☐ Yes ☒ No
If YES - Circle months business will be open:
JAN FEB MAR   APR MAY JUN   JUL AUG SEPT   OCT NOV DEC

M. If an ENTITY (Item C) complete the following:
Date of Incorporation: ___/___/___
month / day / year
State of Incorporation `☐☐`   Fiscal month `☐☐`
NJ Business/Corp. # `☐☐☐☐` `☐☐☐☐`
Is this a Subsidiary of another corporation? ☐ YES ☐ NO
If YES, give name and Federal ID# of parent: _____

N. Standard Industrial Code `☐☐☐☐` (If known)   O. NAICS `☐☐☐☐☐☐` (If known)

P. Provide the following information for the owner, partners or responsible corporate officers. (If more space is needed, attach rider)

OWNERSHIP DETAIL

NAME (Last Name, First, MI)	SOCIAL SECURITY NUMBER / TITLE	HOME ADDRESS (Street, City, State, Zip)	PERCENT OF OWNERSHIP
CARLIN, JON	*111-11-1111* / *PARTNER*	*26 EAST WAY LINCROFT, NJ 07738*	*50*
CARLIN, AMY	*222-22-2222* / *PARTNER*	*26 EAST WAY LINCROFT, NJ 07738*	*50*

BE SURE TO COMPLETE NEXT PAGE

- 17 -

**APPLICATION TO REGISTER A BUSINESS
IN NEW JERSEY
(CONTINUED)**

FEIN#: 22-2222222   NAME: JON AND AMY CARLIN   NJ-REG

Each Question Must Be Answered Completely

1. a. Have you or will you be paying wages, salaries or commissions to employees working in New Jersey within the next 6 months? ☒ Yes ☐ No

   Give date of first wage or salary payment: 1 / 8 / 17
   Month / Day / Year

   If you answered "No" to question 1.a., please be aware that if you begin paying wages you are required to notify the Client Registration Bureau at PO Box 252, Trenton NJ 08646-0252, or phone (609)-292-9292.

   b. Give date of hiring first NJ employee: ___ / ___ / ___
   Month / Day / Year

   c. Date cumulative gross payroll exceeds $1,000   1 / 15 / 17
   Month / Day / Year

   d. Will you be paying wages, salaries or commissions to New Jersey residents working outside New Jersey? .... ☐ Yes ☒ No

   e. Will you be the payer of pension or annuity income to New Jersey residents? .... ☐ Yes ☒ No

   f. Will you be holding legalized games of chance in New Jersey (as defined in Chapter 47 Rules of Legalized Games of Chance) where proceeds from any one prize exceed $1,000? .... ☐ Yes ☒ No

   g. Is this business a PEO (Employee Leasing Company)?   (If yes, see page 6) .... ☐ Yes ☒ No

2. Did you acquire ☐ Substantially all the assets; ☐ Trade or business; ☐ Employees; of any previous employing units? .... ☐ Yes ☒ No
   If answer is "No", go to question 4.
   If answer is "Yes", indicate by a check whether ☐ in whole or ☐ In part, and list business name, address and registration number of predecessor or acquired unit and the date business was acquired by you. (If more than one, list separately. Continue on separate sheet if necessary.)

   Name of Acquired Unit _____   N.J. Employer ID _____

   ACQUIRED   PERCENTAGE ACQUIRED
   ☐ Assets   _____ %
   ☐ Trade or Business   _____ %
   Address _____   Date Acquired _____   ☐ Employees   _____ %

3. Subject to certain regulations, the law provides for the transfer of the predecessor's employment experience to a successor where the whole of a business is acquired from a subject predecessor employer. The transfer of the employment experience is required by law.
   Are the predecessor and successor units owned or controlled by the same interests? .... ☐ Yes ☒ No

4. Is your employment agricultural? .... ☐ Yes ☒ No

5. Is your employment household? .... ☐ Yes ☒ No
   a. If yes, please indicate the date in the calendar quarter in which gross cash wages totaled $1,000 or more ___ / ___ / ___
   Month / Day / Year

6. Are you a 501(c)(3) organization? .... ☐ Yes ☒ No
   If "Yes", to apply for sales tax exemption, obtain form REG-1E at http://www.state.nj.us/treasury/taxation/pdf/other_forms/sales/reg1e.pdf

7. Were you subject to the Federal Unemployment Tax Act (FUTA) in the current or preceding calendar year? .... ☐ Yes ☒ No
   (See instruction sheet for explanation of FUTA.) If "Yes", indicate year: _____

8. a. Does this employing unit claim exemption from liability for contributions under the Unemployment Compensation Law of New Jersey? ..... ☐ Yes ☒ No
   If "Yes," please state reason. (Use additional sheets if necessary.) _____

   b. If exemption from the mandatory provisions of the Unemployment Compensation Law of New Jersey is claimed, does this employing unit wish to voluntarily elect to become subject to its provisions for a period of not less than two complete calendar years? .... ☐ Yes ☐ No

9. Type of business   ☐ 1. Manufacturer   ☐ 2. Service   ☐ 3. Wholesale
                       ☐ 4. Construction   ☒ 5. Retail   ☐ 6. Government

   Principal product or service in New Jersey only BAKED GOODS

   Type of Activity in New Jersey only BAKERY

10. List below each place of business and each class of industry in New Jersey, even though you may have only one place of business or engage in only one class of industry.
    a. Do you have more than one employing facility in New Jersey? .... ☐ Yes ☐ No

NJ WORK LOCATIONS (Physical location, not mailing address)		NATURE OF BUSINESS (See Instructions)			No. of Workers at Each Location and/in Each Class of Industry
Street Address, City, Zip Code	County	NAICS Code	Principal Product or Service Complete Description	%	
44 DONNA COURT CLARK, NJ 07066	UNION	5306	BAKERY	100	1

(Continue on separate sheet, if necessary)

BE SURE TO COMPLETE NEXT PAGE

- 18 -

APPLICATION TO REGISTER A BUSINESS
IN NEW JERSEY
(CONTINUED)

Each Question Must Be Answered Completely

11. a. Will you collect New Jersey Sales Tax and/or pay Use Tax? .... ☒ Yes   ☐ No
    GIVE EXACT DATE YOU EXPECT TO MAKE FIRST SALE   1 / 1 / 17
                                      Month   Day   Year

    b. Will you need to make exempt purchases for your inventory or to produce your product? .... ☒ Yes   ☐ No

    c. Is your business located in (check applicable box(es)):   ☐ Atlantic City   ☐ Salem County
                                            ☐ North Wildwood   ☐ Wildwood Crest   ☐ Wildwood
    d. Do you have more than one location in New Jersey that collects New Jersey Sales Tax? (If yes, see instructions) ...... ☐ Yes   ☒ No

    e. Do you, in the regular course of business, sell, store, deliver or transport natural gas or electricity to users or customers
        in this state whether by mains, lines or pipes located within this State or by any other means of delivery? .... ☐ Yes   ☒ No

12. Do you intend to sell cigarettes? .... ☐ Yes   ☒ No
    Note: If yes, complete the REG-L form on page 45 in this booklet and return with your completed NJ-REG.
         To obtain a cigarette retail or vending machine license complete the form CM-100 on page 48.
13. a. Are you a distributor or wholesaler of tobacco products other than cigarettes? .... ☐ Yes   ☒ No

    b. Do you purchase tobacco products other than cigarettes from outside the State of New Jersey? .... ☐ Yes   ☒ No

14. Are you a manufacturer, wholesaler, distributor or retailer of "litter-generating products"? See instructions for retailer ..... ☐ Yes   ☒ No
    liability and definition of litter-generating products.
15. Are you an owner or operator of a sanitary landfill facility in New Jersey? .... ☐ Yes   ☒ No
    IF YES, indicate D.E.P. Facility # and type (See instructions) _____
16. a. Do you operate a facility that has the total combined capacity to store 200,000 gallons or more of petroleum products? ... ☐ Yes   ☒ No

    b. Do you operate a facility that has the total combined capacity to store 20,000 gallons
        (equals 167,043 pounds) of hazardous chemicals? .... ☐ Yes   ☒ No

    c. Do you store petroleum products or hazardous chemicals at a public storage terminal? .... ☐ Yes   ☒ No
        Name of terminal _____

17. a. Will you be involved with the sale petroleum products? .... ☐ Yes   ☒ No
    Note: If yes, complete the REG-L form in this booklet and return with your completed NJ-REG. You will be sent a motor
         fuel licence application (MFA-1) or you can download this application at www.state.nj.us/treasury/taxation/prntmf.shtml

    b. Will your company be engaged in the refining and/or distributing of petroleum products for distribution in this State or
        the importing of petroleum products into New Jersey for consumption in New Jersey? .... ☐ Yes   ☒ No

    c. Will your business activity require you to issue a Direct Payment Permit in lieu of payment of the Petroleum Products
        Gross Receipts Tax on your purchases of petroleum products? .... ☐ Yes   ☒ No
18. Will you be providing goods and services as a direct contractor or subcontractor to the state, other public agencies
    including local governments, colleges and universities and school boards, or to casino licensees? .... ☐ Yes   ☒ No
19. Will you be engaged in the business of renting motor vehicles for the transportation of persons
    or non-commercial freight? .... ☐ Yes   ☒ No

20. Is your business a hotel, motel, bed & breakfast or similar facility and located in the State of New Jersey? .... ☐ Yes   ☒ No

21. Will this business be operating in the Sports and Entertainment District of Millville NJ ? .... ☐ Yes   ☒ No
    If yes, will the business be engaged in obtaining gross receipts from any of the following (Circle all that apply if "Yes")

  a Sales, rental or leases of tangible personal property b. Sales of food & drink c Charges of admission d Rental charges for hotel occupancies

22. Do you make retail sales of new motor vehicle tires, or sell or lease motor vehicles? .... ☐ Yes   ☒ No

23. Do you provide "cosmetic medical procedures" or goods or occupancies directly associated with such procedures? ...... ☐ Yes   ☒ No
    (See description of Cosmetic Procedures Gross Receipts Tax in the list of Taxes of the State of New Jersey, page 5.)
    Type of Business _____
24. Do you sell voice grade access telecommunications or mobile telecommunications to a customer with a primary
    place of use in this State? .... ☐ Yes   ☒ No
25. Contact Information: Person   AMY CARLIN   Title: PARTNER
    Daytime Phone: (908) 555 - 2738 Ext._____ E-mail address: _ _ _ _ @GMAIL

    Signature of Owner, Partner or Officer: _____

    Title   PARTNER _____ Date: 1-10-17

NO FEE IS REQUIRED TO FILE THIS FORM

> IF YOU ARE A SOLE PROPRIETOR OR A PARTNERSHIP WITHOUT EMPLOYEES - **STOP HERE** -
> IF YOU HAVE EMPLOYEES PROCEED TO THE STATE OF NJ NEW HIRE REPORTING FORM ON PAGE 29

> IF YOU ARE FORMING A CORPORATION, LIMITED LIABILITY COMPANY, LIMITED PARTNERSHIP, OR A LIMITED
> LIABILITY PARTNERSHIP YOU MUST CONTINUE ANSWERING APPLICABLE QUESTIONS ON PAGES 23 AND 24

APPLICATION TO REGISTER A BUSINESS
IN NEW JERSEY
(CONTINUED)

NJ-REG-I INSTRUCTIONS (11-06) BUSINESS REGISTRATION FORM (NJ-REG)

The NJ Division of Revenue adopted this registration procedure to assist you in becoming aware of and understanding all of the taxes and related liabilities to which a new business or applicant for a license may be subject. The procedure covers tax/employer registration for ALL types of businesses, and also covers the filing of NEW legal business entities such as domestic/foreign corporations or limited liability companies (Public Records Filing, page 23-24).

All businesses must complete the registration application (NJ-REG, pages 17-19) in order to receive the forms, returns, instructions, and other information needed to comply with New Jersey laws. This applies to every individual, corporation, or other legal business entity, or unincorporated entity engaged in the conduct or practice of any trade, business, profession, or occupation, whether full time or part time, within the State of New Jersey. Registration requirements also apply to name holder and dormant corporations, as well as to owners of tangible personal property used in business located in New Jersey or leased to another business entity in New Jersey. **Nonprofit "501(c)(3)" or veterans' organizations that need sales tax exemption should complete an REG-1E application; see "Item A" below for details.** Persons commencing business or opening additional places of business must register at least 15 business days prior to commencement or opening. There is no fee for filing NJ-REG; however, as outlined in the instructions, there are fees for filing new business entities.

Mail the completed NJ-REG to:	Overnight Delivery of NJ-REG to:
NEW JERSEY DIVISION OF REVENUE	NEW JERSEY DIVISION OF REVENUE
PO BOX 252	847 ROEBLING AVENUE
TRENTON, NEW JERSEY 08646-0252	TRENTON, NJ 08611

To submit a Public Records Filing or combined Public Records Filing with NJ-REG, refer to page 21 (Items 2 a-c).

IMPORTANT- READ THE FOLLOWING INSTRUCTIONS CAREFULLY BEFORE COMPLETING ANY FORMS. PRINT OR TYPE ALL INFORMATION. PROVIDE A COMPLETE APPLICATION. FAILURE TO PROPERLY COMPLETE THE APPLICATION MAY DELAY ISSUANCE OF YOUR CERTIFICATE OF AUTHORITY OR LICENSE.

PAGE 17 INSTRUCTIONS

Item A Check the appropriate box to indicate reason for filing the application. Nonprofits that are 501(c)(3), volunteer fire, veterans' or PTO organizations and need sales tax exemption file Form REG-1E. The REG-1E (including Q & A's) is available through the Forms Request System at 800-323-4400 or 609-826-4400 (choose option 4, then 9); or at www.state.nj.us/treasury/taxation/exemption.htm.

Item B Enter the FEIN assigned to the employer or vendor by the Internal Revenue Service or if not required, enter the Social Security Number assigned to the sole proprietor. Check the box if you have applied for your FEIN.

Item C Enter the corporate name of the business being registered or the name(s) of the owner(s) if an individual or partnership.

Item D Enter the Trade Name, if different from Item C.

Item E Enter the address of the **physical** location of the business, do not use a PO Box address. Be sure to include the **nine-digit zip-code.**

Item F Enter the name and address to which **all** New Jersey tax returns will be mailed. Be sure to include the nine-digit zip code. If you wish different type tax returns to go to different addresses, please attach a separate sheet and indicate the address to which each tax return is to go.

Item G Enter the date which you started or assumed ownership of this business in New Jersey. If your business has not yet started, enter the date that you will commence doing business. If no business is conducted in NJ, but, you are going to withhold NJ Gross Income Tax for employees, enter the date withholding will begin. Use today's date if you only need a Business Registration Certificate.

Item H Check the appropriate box for your Type of Ownership. If you check "S Corporation," complete the New Jersey S Corporation Election form (CBT-2553) found in this booklet on page 41.

Item I Enter your New Jersey Business Code from Table A. If you are engaged in more than one type of business, enter the code for the predominant one. **This section must be completed to avoid delays in issuance of the Certificate of Authority or License.**

Item J Enter your New Jersey County/Municipality Code from Table B. This code reflects the County/Municipality in which your business is located.

Item K Enter the county where your business is located.

Item L If this business will be open all year, check **NO**. If this is a seasonal business, check the **"YES"** box and circle the months the business will be OPEN.

Item M If the business is a corporation, enter the date and state of

incorporation, the fiscal month of the corporation and the NJ corporation business number of the corporation. If this business is a subsidiary of another corporation, check "YES" and enter the name and FEIN of the parent.

Item N Enter the four-digit Standard Industrial Code (SIC) if known.

Item O Enter the six-digit North American Industrial Classification System Code (NAICS) if known. (See Table C, page 14)

Item P Enter the names of the owner, partners or responsible corporate officer(s). Enter the social security number, title, and home address for each person listed.

PAGE 18 INSTRUCTIONS -

Question 1:

(a) Have you or will you be paying wages, salaries or commissions to employees working in New Jersey within the next 6 months, check "YES" and enter the date of the first payment. This date must be provided for Unemployment and Disability registration purposes. If "NO", please be aware that if you begin paying wages you are required to notify the Client Registration Bureau at (609)-292-1730.

(b) If 1(a) is "YES", enter the date you hired your 1st New Jersey employee.

(c) This date must be provided for Unemployment and Disability registration purposes. Accumulate the gross periodic payrolls until they add up to a total of $1,000. Enter that date on line 1c.

(d) If you will be paying wages, salaries or commissions to New Jersey residents working outside New Jersey, check "YES".

(e) If you will be the payer of pensions and/or annuities to New Jersey residents, check "YES" and enter the date of the first payment.

(f) If you will be holding legalized games of chance in New Jersey (as defined in Chapter 47 "Rules of Legalized Games of Chance") where proceeds from any one prize exceed $1,000, check "YES" and enter the date of the first prize awarded. (NJ Lottery proceeds are not included.)

(g) A PEO (Employee Leasing Company) that registers with the NJ Division of Revenue via NJ-REG is subject to an additional and separate registration process with the **NJ Department of Labor**. To obtain the special PEO registration forms and information, please visit our website, www.state.nj.us/labor/ea/eaindex.html or call 609-633-6400 x 2209.

Question 2:

If you purchased or otherwise came into possession of 90% or more of the assets of another business, check "Substantially all the assets". If you purchased or otherwise received the right to continue to operate the entire trade or business of another employer, check "Trade or Business". If you took over all the employees of an existing business, excluding corporate officers if any, check "Employees".

INSTRUCTIONS FOR
APPLICATION TO REGISTER A BUSINESS
IN NEW JERSEY

Enter the name, any trade name and address of the business you acquired. Also enter the New Jersey Unemployment Registration Number or FEIN of the prior business as well as the date you purchased the business. Also indicate the percentage of assets, trade or business and employees that you took over from the prior business.

Question 3:
When the successor acquires or absorbs and continues the business of a subject predecessor, the successor employer must receive the transfer of the predecessor's employment experience. The transfer of employment experience is required by law.

Question 4: Agricultural labor means the following activities:

1. Services performed on a farm in connection with cultivation of the soil; raising or harvesting any agricultural or horticultural product; raising, feeding, caring for and managing livestock, bees, poultry or fur-bearing animals; handling, packaging, or processing any agricultural or horticultural commodity in its unmanufactured state; repair and maintenance of equipment or real property used in the agricultural activity; and transport of agricultural or horticultural supplies or products if not in the usual course of a trucking business;

2. Service performed in a greenhouse or nursery if over 50 percent of the gross sales volume is attributable to products raised in the greenhouse or nursery; and

3. Service performed by a cooperative of which the producer of the agricultural product is a member if the service performed is incidental and necessary to the delivery of the product to market in a finished state.

   Agricultural labor does not include:
   1. Service performed at a race track;
   2. Service in the breeding, care or boarding of domesticated animals of a kind normally found in a home, such as dogs and cats;
   3. Service in a retail enterprise selling the product of an agricultural enterprise if the retail enterprise is not located on or contiguous to the site of production; or
   4. Service in a retail enterprise located on or contiguous to the site of production if greater than 50% of the gross sales volume of the retail enterprise is attributable to items not produced at the site.

Question 5:
Household service means service of a personal nature performed outside of a business enterprise for a householder. Household service is normally performed in a private residence, but may be performed in other settings such as a nursing home or a yacht. Household service would include, but is not limited to, the following occupations: maids, butlers, cooks, valets, gardeners, chauffeurs; personal secretaries, baby-sitters and nurses' aides.

   (a) If "YES", this date is to be provided for Unemployment and Disability registration purposes. Accumulate the gross periodic cash payrolls until they add up to a total of $1,000 in a calendar quarter. Enter that date here.

Question 6:
Has the Internal Revenue Service determined that your organization is exempt from income tax as a 501(c)(3) organization? If yes, check "YES".

Question 7:
Any employing unit subject to the provisions of the Federal Unemployment Tax Act (FUTA) in the current or preceding calendar year automatically becomes an employer unless services are specifically excluded under the New Jersey Unemployment Law. An employing unit (other than one which employs agricultural workers) is generally subject to FUTA if it had covered employment during some portion of a day in 20 different calendar weeks within the calendar year or had a quarterly payroll of $1,500 or more.

Question 8:
If you believe that you or your business is not required to pay unemployment and temporary disability contributions on wages paid to its employees, check "YES", otherwise check "NO". Examples are: This is a church or the only employees of this proprietorship are the spouse and children under age 18. You may be subject to New Jersey Gross Income Tax Withholding.

Question 9:
For principal product or service in New Jersey only, please provide a description for that product or service which accounts for over 50% of your business (e.g. fuel oil). Please briefly describe the type of activity your business is engaged in (e.g. drive a fuel truck to sell fuel oil to consumers).

Question 10:
This information is to be supplied by every employer regardless of the number of work locations in New Jersey or the number of classes of industry which it is engaged in. Please do not describe work location by post office box number. The incorporated municipalities in which workers operate or to which they report daily should be named instead. If there is more than one location please list each location beginning with the largest employing facility first. Please provide the location address and indicate the nature of business conducted at each location. If two or more principal classes of activity are conducted at one location, please indicate.

In describing the "Nature of Business", classify your "Primary Activity" under one of the following: wholesale trade, retail trade, manufacturing, mining and quarrying, construction (general or specific), real estate, insurance, finance, transportation, communication, or other public utilities, personal service. business service, professional service, agriculture, forestry, fishery. If the employing unit is engaged in trade, state under "Primary Activity" whether as wholesaler, commission merchant or wholesale branch of manufacturing concern, retailer (store, route, restaurant, fast food, service station, and the like), or retail branch of manufacturing concern. Please refer to the list of business codes provided.

For units engaged in manufacturing, state the product which has the greatest gross annual value. Describe also the basic raw materials or articles. For units with more than one principal product or service show percentage of gross value in each.

For contractors (subcontractors) in construction, state the type of activity, such as general (building or other), highway, heavy marine (not ship), water well, demolition, or specific (i.e. plumbing, painting, masonry or stone, carpentry, roofing, concrete, general maintenance construction, etc.), speculative builder, development builder.

For service providers, state whether hotel, laundry, photography, barber or beauty, funeral, garment, hygienic, business janitor, news, radio, accounting, educational, repair, entertainment, amusement, athletic specific professional, etc.

For the wholesaler or retailer, describe primary commodity.

If engaged in marine transportation, state whether on inland water-ways, harbors, coastwise or trans-oceanic.

For employers engaged in more than one business activity (i.e. service station, mini-mart) show (in the percent column) the relative gross business each activity does.

The average number of employees on the payroll at each location and in each class of activity should be shown. Please continue on a separate sheet if needed.

PAGE 19 INSTRUCTIONS
Question 11

   (a) If you will be collecting New Jersey Sales Tax and/or paying Use Tax check "YES" and enter the date of the first sale.
   (b) Check "YES" if you will be making tax exempt purchases. If "YES", you will be issued New Jersey Resale Certificates (ST-3) and/or Exempt Use Certificates (ST-4).

      NOTE: Form ST-3, Resale Certificate. Issued to a vendor by a purchaser who is not the "end user" of the goods or services being purchased.

      Form ST-4, Exempt Use Certificate. Issued to a vendor by a purchaser who is purchasing goods for an exempt use.

   (c) If your business is located within Atlantic City, Salem County, North Wildwood, Wildwood Crest or Wildwood, check the applicable box.

      If you are eligible for the New York/New Jersey Cooperative Interstate Sales Tax Agreement, indicate this in Question 18 under "Other State Taxes."

   (d) All NJ locations collecting NJ sales tax must be registered. If "YES", attach a rider requesting consolidated reporting.

   (e) If you sell, store, deliver or transport natural gas or electricity to users or customers whether by mains, lines, or pipes located within this State or by any other means of delivery, check "YES.

- 7 -

2, 7

INSTRUCTIONS FOR
APPLICATION TO REGISTER A BUSINESS
IN NEW JERSEY
(CONTINUED)

Question 12:
If you intend to sell cigarettes in New Jersey, check "YES." If "YES," complete Form REG-L if you are requesting a wholesaler, distributor or manufacturer license application. Complete Form CM-100 if you are applying for a retailer or vending machine license. You will be sent the appropriate license/license application after these forms are processed.

Question 13:
(a) If you are a distributor or wholesaler of tobacco products other than cigarettes, check "YES." Examples of tobacco products are: cigars, little cigars, cigarillos, chewing tobacco, pipe tobacco, smoking tobacco, tobacco substitutes and snuff. Cigarettes are exempt from the Tobacco Products Wholesale Sales and Use Tax.

(b) If the distributor or wholesaler has not collected the Tobacco Products Wholesale Sales and Use Tax from the retailer or consumer, the retailer or consumer is responsible for remitting the compensating use tax on the price paid or charged directly to the Division of Taxation within 20 days of the date the tax was required to be paid.

Question 14:
If you are a manufacturer, wholesaler, distributor or retailer of "litter-generating products, check "YES." Litter-generating products are: food, soft drinks and carbonated water, beer, wine, distilled spirits, glass containers, metal containers, plastic or fiber containers, groceries, drugstore sundries, cigarettes and tobacco products, motor vehicle tires, newsprint and magazine paper stock, paper products and household paper, and cleaning agents and toiletries.

Question 15:
If you are an owner or operator of a sanitary landfill facility in New Jersey, check "YES" and indicate the facility number and type as classified by the New Jersey Department of Environmental Protection. Registration instructions for the Solid Waste Services and Landfill Closure and Contingency taxes will be forwarded.

Question 16:
(a) If you operate a facility that has the total combined capacity to store 200,000 gallons or more of petroleum products, check "YES."

(b) If you operate a facility that has the total combined capacity to store 20,000 gallons of hazardous chemicals, check "YES."

(c) If you store petroleum products or hazardous chemicals at a public storage terminal, check "YES," and enter the name of the terminal. A Spill Compensation and Control Tax registration application will be forwarded.

Question 17
(a) If your company will be involved with the sale or transport of motor fuels and/or petroleum, check "YES." If "YES," complete Form REG-L if you are requesting a wholesaler, distributor, import, export, seller/use, gasoline jobber, or storage facility operator license application. Complete CM-100 if you are applying for a retail dealer or transport license. You will be sent the appropriate license/license application after these forms are processed.

(b) If your company is engaged in refining and/or distributing petroleum products for distribution in this State, or importing petroleum products into New Jersey for consumption in New Jersey, check "YES." If you have checked "YES," complete Form REG-L and return it with your competed NJ-REG.

(c) If you checked "YES," you will be sent a Direct Payment Permit application.

Question 18:
If you will be providing goods or services to casino licensees or acting as a contractor or subcontractor to the State or its agencies, check the "YES" box.

Question 19:
Businesses involved in the rental of motor vehicles (less than 28 day agreements), including passenger autos, trucks and trailers designed for use on the highways, other than those used for the transportation of commercial freight, are subject to the payment of a $2 per day Domestic Security Fee. If eligible, a business must check YES and go to http://www.state.nj.us/treasury/taxation/prntmisc.htm for instructions on how to report and pay the fee quarterly either electronically or by phone (Form DSF-100). See Technical Bulletin 47(R) on this topic at: http://www.state.nj.us/treasury/taxation/publtb.htm.

Question 20:
Businesses engaged in the rental of rooms in a hotel, motel, bed & breakfast or similar facility are required to collect a State Occupancy Fee of 5% as of 7-1-04. In addition, a Municipal Occupancy Tax of up to 3% must also be collected, if enacted by the municipality where the facility is located. If such a facility, check YES. You will receive the HM-100 return, which must be filed with payment by the 20th of each month. For additional information on the Fee and a list of municipalities that have enacted the Tax, go to: http://www.state.nj.us/treasury/taxation/hotelfeeinfo.htm.

Question 21:
Businesses that hold an outdoor advertising license or permit issued by the New Jersey DOT are subject to the 6% Outdoor Advertising Fee imposed on gross amounts collected for the sale of advertising space. If you have such a license or permit, check YES. You will receive the OA-100 return which is due on a quarterly basis. For additional information on the Fee, go to: www.state.nj.us/treasury/taxation.

Question 22:
If you sell new tires, or sell or lease motor vehicles, you must check YES. You will receive information regarding the collection of the Motor Vehicle Tire Fee.

Question 23:
If you provide such services, check YES and indicate the type of business, service or practice you are engaged in (e.g. plastic surgery, electrolysis, beauty salon/spa, hair replacement facility, hospital)

Question 24:
If you are a telephone exchange company or a mobile telecommunications carrier which provides voice grade access telephone numbers or service lines as part of that telephone exchange service, thereby providing access to 9-1-1 service through the public switched network, you must check YES. You will receive the ERF-100 return which is due on a quarterly basis.

Question 25:
"Fur clothing" means an item that satisfies the following criteria: Its sale is exempt from sales tax under the "clothing" exemption of the Sales and Use Tax Act and fur is a chief component of its value. "Fur" means fur on the hide or pelt of an animal.

Question 26:
Contact Person: Enter the name, title, telephone number and e-mail address of the contact person who will answer questions regarding the registration application.

Signature: The application **must be signed and dated** by the owner if a sole proprietorship, or in the case of a corporation, by the president, vice-president, secretary, treasurer, comptroller, or other duly authorized officer. Unsigned applications cannot be processed and will be returned.

INSTRUCTIONS FOR
APPLICATION TO REGISTER A BUSINESS
IN NEW JERSEY
(CONTINUED)

TABLE A - NEW JERSEY BUSINESS CODES

Enter one of the following four-digit numbers in Block I to indicate the product group or service of your business:

MISCELLANEOUS WITHHOLDER CODES

Code	Description
2781	Pension Plan Withholders
2779	Employer of Domestic Household Employees

MANUFACTURING BUSINESS CODES

Code	Description
1631	Aircraft and Related Supplies
1314	Alcoholic Beverages/Liquor
1100	Apparel
1404	Appliances, Housewares, Linens
1622	Art, Mechanical Drawing & Related Supplies
1815	Asphalt
1405	Audio/Visual (TV, Stereo, Records, CD)
1208	Auto Parts and Related Products/Accessories
1220	Auto Windows/Glass
1200	Automotive
1306	Baked Goods
1637	Bicycles and Related Merchandise
1604	Books, Magazines, Periodicals, Newspapers
1316	Bottled Water
1809	Building Materials and Supplies
1800	Building/Construction
1213	Buses, Bus Parts
1614	Cameras, Photo Equipment and Supplies
1304	Candy, Nuts and Confectionery
1104	Children's & Infants' Clothing and/or Accessories
1602	Computer Hardware, Software
1808	Concrete
1627	Containers (Industrial/Commercial)
1110	Costumes
1107	Custom Clothing and Tailoring
1305	Dairy Products
1601	Drugs & Medical Supplies, Medical Equipment
1502	Dry Goods
1903	Electric
1905	Electric and Gas
1804	Electrical Materials
1630	Electronic Equipment
1812	Energy Conservation Related
1105	Family Clothing
1607	Farm and Garden Equipment and Supplies
1823	Fencing
1611	Flowers and Related Merchandise
1300	Food
1106	Footwear
1103	Formal Wear (Tuxedos, Bridal Gowns, etc.)
1303	Fruit and/or Vegetables
1609	Fuel (Bottled Gas, Kerosene, Charcoal, etc.)
1400	Furniture
1108	Furriers
1904	Gas
1500	General Merchandise
1615	Gifts, Souvenirs
1301	Grocery Items
1634	Hair Grooming Supplies
1813	Hardware
1315	Health Food Products
1810	Heating, Ventilation and Air Conditioning
1401	Household Furniture and Furnishings
1610	Ice
1311	Ice Cream Products
1619	Industrial Supplies
1618	Industrial Tools and Equipment, Machinery
1820	Iron and Steel
1608	Jewelry
1406	Lamps, Lights, Shades
1617	Leather Goods and Luggage
1814	Lumber
1302	Meat and /or Fish
1101	Men's and Boys' Clothing and/or Accessories
1111	Millinery and Accessories
1626	Miscellaneous Decorative & Display Materials
1600	Miscellaneous Products
1621	Models and Hobby Related Merchandise
1638	Monuments, Caskets & Related Merchandise
1201	Motor Vehicles
1207	Motorboats
1209	Motorcycles, Minibikes
1215	Mufflers
1606	Musical Instruments & Related Merchandise
1318	Non-Alcoholic Beverages
1402	Office Furniture and Furnishings
1616	Optical Goods
1803	Paint, Wallpaper and Decorating
1633	Paintings, Sculpture and Related Artwork
1628	Paper and Packaging Products
1635	Perfumes and Cosmetics
1640	Pet Supplies
1313	Pizza
1802	Plumbing Materials
1623	Pools and Related Accessories
1202	Recreational Vehicles, Campers
1807	Roofing Materials
1822	Siding (Aluminum, Brickface, Stucco)
1620	Signs and Advertising Displays
1636	Soaps, Detergents, etc.
1307	Specialty Foods
1605	Sporting Goods and Related Merchandise
1603	Stamps, Coins, Gold, Precious Metals, etc.
1613	Stationery, Greeting Cards, School Supplies
1906	Steam
1902	Telegraph
1901	Telephone
1624	Telephones, Telecommunications Equipment
1625	Textiles and Related Products
1629	Tile and Ceramic Merchandise
1203	Tires
1612	Tobacco Products
1632	Toys and Games
1210	Trailers
1214	Transmissions
1212	Trucks, Truck Parts
1109	Uniforms
1900	Utilities
1907	Water
1816	Well Drilling, Water Pumps
1811	Windows, Doors, Glass
1102	Women's & Girls' Clothing and/or Accessories

SERVICE BUSINESS CODES

Code	Description
2740	Accounting
2720	Advertising, Public Relations
2631	Aircraft and Related Supplies
2778	Alcoholic Beverage Pick-up & Transport
2775	Apartments, Condominiums, Homeowner Association
2100	Apparel
2404	Appliances, Housewares
2769	Appraising
2741	Architecture & Engineering Services
2717	Athletic Club (Spas, Gyms, etc.)
2405	Audio/Visual (TV, Stereo, Records, CD)
2217	Auto Body, Painting
2219	Auto Salvage/Junk Yard
2218	Auto Upholstery, Vinyl
2220	Auto Windows/Glass
2205	Automobiles
2200	Automotive
2705	Banks
2637	Bicycles & Related Merchandise
2213	Buses
2751	Cable TV
2614	Cameras, Photo Equipment & Supplies
2216	Car Wash & Wax
2767	Casino/Casino Hotel
2317	Catering
2764	Cemeteries, Crematories
2744	Charter Fishing

Code	Description
2711	Coin Operated Laundries
2602	Computer Hardware, Software
2754	Consulting Services (All Types)
2107	Custom Clothing & Tailoring
2761	Data Processing
2709	Dry Cleaning
2708	Duplicating, Photocopying
2903	Electric
2905	Electric and Gas
2630	Electronic Equipment
2779	Employer of Domestic/Household Employees
2745	Employment Agencies
2715	Entertainment (Amusement, Circus, Movies, & Sports)
2718	Equipment Rental/Leasing
2607	Farm & Garden Equipment & Supplies
2300	Food
2106	Footwear
2737	Funeral Services
2400	Furniture
2904	Gas
2204	Gasoline Service Station
2736	Governmental Services
2749	Graphics
2762	Hair Salons, Hair Dressers, Barber Shops
2752	Health Clubs/Programs (Exercise, Tanning, Diet)
2759	Hospitals, Clinics, Institutions
2701	Hotels & Motels
2768	Import/Export
2618	Industrial Tools & Equipment, Machinery
2755	Instructions (Dancing, Driving, etc.)
2732	Insurance
2729	Interior Cleaning/Janitorial, Rug Cleaning
2756	Interior Decorator
2742	Investment/Financial Services (Pension Plans)
2608	Jewelry
2725	Junk Dealers
2721	Landscaping, Lawn Service, Gardening
2617	Leather Goods and Luggage
2726	Linen Service & Rentals
2771	Locksmith
2728	Marinas, Boat & Dock Rentals, Bait
2730	Marine Maintenance & Repairs
2601	Medical Equipment
2600	Miscellaneous Products
2700	Miscellaneous Service
2753	Modeling Agencies
2621	Models & Hobby Related merchandise
2638	Monuments, Caskets & Related Merchandise
2201	Motor Vehicle Dealers (New and/or Used Autos)
2207	Motorboats
2209	Motorcycles, Minibikes
2215	Mufflers
2606	Musical Instruments & Related Merchandise
2719	Nursery, Day Care, Camps
2747	Nursing Homes & Convalescent Centers
2616	Optical Goods
2731	Organizations (Scouts, Fraternal, etc.)
2758	Parking/Parking Lots
2757	Participating Sports (Golf, Bowling, etc.)
2727	Pawn Brokers
2710	Pest Control
2723	Pet Grooming, Boarding, Training, Breeding
2707	Photo Printing & Processing
2706	Photographic, Sound Studios
2623	Pools & Related Accessories
2714	Printing and Publishing
2739	Professional Legal Services
2738	Professional Medical Services, Health Care
2704	Public Warehousing/Storage
2712	Radio and TV Repair

INSTRUCTIONS FOR
APPLICATION TO REGISTER A BUSINESS
IN NEW JERSEY
(CONTINUED)

Code	Description	Code	Description	Code	Description
2733	Real Estate	3105	Family Clothing	3900	Utilities
2202	Recreational Vehicles, Campers	3607	Farm & Garden Equipment & Supplies	3907	Water
2776	Recycling Related	3823	Fencing	3816	Well Drilling, Water Pumps
2401	Refinishing, Upholstery, etc.	3611	Flowers & Related Merchandise	3811	Windows, Doors, Glass
2702	Rooming & Boarding Houses	3300	Food	3102	Women's & Girls' Clothing and/or Accessories
2748	Safe Deposit Boxes (Post Office, Bank)	3106	Footwear		
2750	Security Services, Alarms	3103	Formal Wear (Tuxedos, Bridal Gowns, etc.)		**CONSTRUCTION BUSINESS CODES**
2773	Shipping & Mailing, Couriers	3303	Fruit and/or Vegetables	4815	Asphalt
2620	Signs & Advertising Displays	3609	Fuel (Bottled Gas, Kerosene, Charcoal, etc.)	4800	Building
2765	Snow Removal	3400	Furniture	4806	Carpentering & Wood Flooring
2716	Social Club (Dating, etc.)	3108	Furriers	4808	Concrete Work
2605	Sporting Goods & Related Merchandise	3904	Gas	4817	Demolition, Excavation
2906	Steam	3500	General Merchandise	4821	Dry Wall, Plaster
2770	Surveying	3615	Gifts, Souvenirs	4804	Electrical Work
2902	Telegraph	3301	Grocery Items	4812	Energy Conservation
2901	Telephone	3634	Hair Grooming Supplies	4823	Fencing
2624	Telephones, Telecommunications Equipment	3813	Hardware	4801	General Building Contractor
2203	Tires	3315	Health Food Products	4810	Heating & Air Conditioning
2211	Towing	3810	Heating, Ventilation & Air Conditioning	4820	Iron & Steel
2632	Toys & Games	3401	Household Furniture & Furnishings	4805	Masonry & Stonework
2703	Trailer Parks & Camps	3610	Ice	4818	Miscellaneous Construction & Repair
2210	Trailers	3311	Ice Cream Products	4803	Painting, Paper Hanging & Decorating
2214	Transmissions	3619	Industrial Supplies	4802	Plumbing
2734	Transportation (Limousines, Chauffeurs, Taxis, Buses)	3618	Industrial Tools & Equipment, Machinery	4807	Roofing
		3820	Iron & Steel	4819	Septic & Cesspool
2724	Trash Removal	3608	Jewelry	4822	Siding (Aluminum, Brickface, Stucco)
2722	Travel Agencies	3406	Lamps, Lights, Shades	4816	Well Drilling
2743	Trucking and Moving	3617	Leather Goods & Luggage	4811	Windows, Doors, Glass
2212	Trucks	3814	Lumber		
2763	Unions	3302	Meat and/or Fish		**RETAIL BUSINESS CODES**
2713	Upholstery & Furniture Repair, Refinishing	3101	Men's & Boys' Clothing and/or Accessories	5631	Aircraft & Related Supplies
2900	Utilities	3111	Millinery & Accessories	5314	Alcoholic Beverages/Liquor
2774	Valet	3626	Miscellaneous Decorative & Display Materials	5508	Annual Shows
2760	Veterinarians, Animal Hospitals	3600	Miscellaneous Products	5100	Apparel
2772	Video Rentals & Related	3621	Models & Hobby Related Merchandise	5404	Appliances, Housewares, Linens
2907	Water	3638	Monuments, Caskets & Related Merchandise	5622	Art, Mechanical Drawing & Related Supplies
2777	Water Systems Related (Purification, Pumps, etc.)	3201	Motor Vehicles	5815	Asphalt
		3207	Motorboats	5405	Audio/Visual (TV, Stereo, Records, CD, etc.)
2766	Welding	3209	Motorcycles, Minibikes	5208	Auto Parts and Related Products/Accessories
2735	Window Washing	3215	Mufflers	5218	Auto Upholstery, Vinyl
2746	Word Processing, Typing, Addressing, etc.	3606	Musical Instruments & Related Merchandise	5220	Auto Windows/Glass
		3318	Non-Alcoholic Beverages	5219	Automobile Junk/Scrap Yard
	WHOLESALE BUSINESS CODES	3402	Office Furniture & Furnishings	5206	Automobile Rentals and Leasing
3631	Aircraft & Relates Supplies	3616	Optical Goods	5200	Automotive
3314	Alcoholic Beverages/Liquor	3803	Paint, Wallpaper & Decorating	5306	Bakeries
3100	Apparel	3633	Paintings, Sculpture & Related Artwork	5309	Bars, Taverns, Pubs
3404	Appliances, Housewares, Linens	3628	Paper & Packaging Products	5637	Bicycles and Related Merchandise
3622	Art, Mechanical Drawing & Related Supplies	3635	Perfumes & Cosmetics	5604	Books, Magazines, Periodicals, Newspapers
3815	Asphalt	3640	Pet Supplies	5316	Bottled Water
3405	Audio/Visual (TV, Stereo, Records, DC, etc.)	3313	Pizza	5800	Building
3208	Auto Parts & Related Products/Accessories	3802	Plumbing Materials	5809	Building Materials and Supplies
3220	Auto Windows/Glass	3623	Pools & Related Accessories	5213	Buses, Bus Parts
3200	Automotive	3202	Recreational Vehicles, Campers	5614	Cameras, Photo Equipment and Supplies
3306	Baked Goods	3639	Religious Articles, Clothing & Related	5304	Candy, Nuts and Confectionery
3637	Bicycles & Related Merchandise	3807	Roofing Materials	5317	Catering
3604	Books, Magazines, Periodicals, Newspapers	3403	Second Hand Items/Antiques	5104	Children's & Infants' Clothing and/or Accessories
3316	Bottled Water	3822	Siding (Aluminum, Brickface, Stucco)		
3809	Building Materials & Supplies	3620	Signs & Advertising Displays	5641	Collectors Items (Baseball Cards, Comics, etc.)
3800	Building/Construction	3636	Soaps, Detergents, etc.	5602	Computer Hardware, Software
3213	Buses, Bus Parts	3307	Specialty Foods	5808	Concrete
3614	Cameras, Photo Equipment & Supplies	3605	Sporting Goods & Related Merchandise	5627	Containers (Industrial/Commercial)
3304	Candy, Nuts & Confectionery	3603	Stamps, Coins, Gold, Precious Metals, etc.	5110	Costumes
3104	Children's & Infants' Clothing and/or Acces.	3613	Stationery, Greeting Cards, School Supplies	5107	Custom Clothing and Tailoring
3602	Computer Hardware, Software	3906	Steam	5305	Dairy Products
3808	Concrete	3902	Telegraph	5501	Department Store
3627	Containers (Industrial/Commercial)	3901	Telephone	5506	Direct Selling Organization (Amway, etc.)
3110	Costumes	3624	Telephones, Telecommunications Equipment	5601	Drugs and Medical Supplies, Medical Equipment
3305	Dairy Products	3625	Textiles & Related Products		
3601	Drugs & Medical Supplies, Medical Equipment	3629	Tile & Ceramic Merchandise	5502	Dry Goods and General Merchandise
3502	Dry Goods	3203	Tires	5804	Electrical Materials
3903	Electric	3612	Tobacco Products	5630	Electronic Equipment
3905	Electric & Gas	3632	Toys & Games	5812	Energy Conservation Related
3804	Electrical Materials	3210	Trailers	5105	Family Clothing
3630	Electronic Equipment	3214	Transmissions	5607	Farm and Garden Equipment and Supplies
3812	Energy Conservation Related	3212	Trucks, Truck Parts		
		3109	Uniforms		

INSTRUCTIONS FOR
APPLICATION TO REGISTER A BUSINESS
IN NEW JERSEY
(CONTINUED)

TABLE A - NEW JERSEY BUSINESS CODES (continued)

Enter one of the following four-digit numbers in Block I to indicate the product group or service of your business:

Code	Description	Code	Description	Code	Description
5312	Fast Food (Burgers, Chicken, Hot Dogs, Tacos, etc.)	5504	Limited Price Variety Store	5202	Recreational Vehicles, Campers
5823	Fencing	5814	Lumber	5639	Religious Articles, Clothing and Related
5507	Flea Markets	5503	Mail Order House	5310	Restaurants (With Liquor)
5611	Flowers and Related Merchandise	5302	Meat and Fish	5308	Restaurants, Diners, Eateries (No Liquor)
5300	Food	5101	Men's and Boy's Clothing and/or Accessories	5807	Roofing Materials
5106	Footwear	5505	Merchandise Vending Machine Operator	5403	Second Hand Items/Antiques
5103	Formal Wear (Tuxedos, Bridal Gowns)	5111	Millinery and Accessories	5822	Siding
5303	Fruit and Vegetables, Produce Stands	5626	Miscellaneous Decorative & Display Materials	5620	Signs and Advertising Displays
5609	Fuel (Bottled Gas, Kerosene, Charcoal, etc.)	5600	Miscellaneous Products	5636	Soaps, Detergents, etc.
5400	Furniture	5621	Models and Hobby Related Merchandise	5307	Specialty Foods (Charles Chips)
5108	Furriers	5638	Monuments, Caskets & Related Merchandise	5605	Sporting Goods and Related Merchandise
5500	General Merchandise	5201	Motor Vehicle Dealers (New and /or Used Autos)	5603	Stamps, Coins, Gold, Precious Metals, etc.
5615	Gifts, Souvenirs			5613	Stationery, Greeting Cards, School Supplies
5301	Groceries Including Delicatessens	5207	Motorboats	5624	Telephones, Telecommunications Equipment
5634	Hair Grooming Supplies	5209	Motorcycles, Minibikes	5625	Textiles and Related Products
5813	Hardware	5215	Mufflers	5629	Tile and Ceramic Merchandise
5315	Health Foods	5606	Musical Instruments and Related Merchandise	5203	Tires
5810	Heating, Ventilation & Air Conditioning	5318	Non-Alcoholic Beverages	5612	Tobacco Products
5401	Household Furniture & Furnishings	5402	Office Furniture, Equipment and Supplies	5632	Toys and Games
5610	Ice	5616	Optical Goods	5210	Trailers
5311	Ice Cream Products	5803	Paint, Wallpaper	5214	Transmissions
5619	Industrial Supplies	5633	Paintings, Sculpture and Related Artwork	5212	Trucks, Truck Parts
5618	Industrial Tools and Equipment, Machinery	5628	Paper and Packaging Products	5109	Uniforms
5820	Iron and Steel	5635	Perfumes and Cosmetics	5816	Well Drilling, Water Pumps
5608	Jewelry	5640	Pet Supplies	5811	Windows, Doors, Glass
5406	Lamps, Lights, Shades	5313	Pizzerias	5102	Women's and Girl's Clothing and/or Accessories
5617	Leather Goods and Luggage	5802	Plumbing Materials		
		5623	Pools and Related Accessories		

INSTRUCTIONS FOR
APPLICATION TO REGISTER A BUSINESS
IN NEW JERSEY
(CONTINUED)

TABLE B - NEW JERSEY COUNTY / MUNICIPALITY CODES

Enter the Appropriate Four-Digit Number in the Boxes Provided on Page 17, Item J.

Location Code	Municipality
ATLANTIC COUNTY	
0101	Absecon City
0102	Atlantic City
0103	Brigantine City
0104	Buena Bor.
0105	Buena Vista Twp.
0106	Corbin City City
0107	Egg Harbor City
0108	Egg Harbor Twp.
0109	Estell Manor City
0110	Folsom Bor.
0111	Galloway Twp.
0112	Hamilton Twp.
0113	Hammonton Town
0114	Linwood City
0115	Longport Bor.
0116	Margate City
0117	Mullica Twp.
0118	Northfield City
0119	Pleasantville City
0120	Port Republic City
0121	Somers Point City
0122	Ventnor City
0123	Weymouth Twp.
BERGEN COUNTY	
0201	Allendale Bor.
0202	Alpine Bor.
0203	Bergenfield Bor.
0204	Bogota Bor.
0205	Carlstadt Bor.
0206	Cliffside Park Bor.
0207	Closter Bor.
0208	Cresskill Bor.
0209	Demarest Bor.
0210	Dumont Bor.
0211	Elmwood Park Bor.
0212	East Rutherford Bor.
0213	Edgewater Bor.
0214	Emerson Bor.
0215	Englewood City
0216	Englewood Cliffs Bor.
0217	Fair Lawn Bor.
0218	Fairview Bor.
0219	Fort Lee Bor.
0220	Franklin Lakes Bor.
0221	Garfield City
0222	Glen Rock Bor.
0223	Hackensack City
0224	Harrington Park Bor.
0225	Hasbrouck Heights Bor.
0226	Haworth Bor.
0227	Hillsdale Bor.
0228	Hohokus Bor.
0229	Leonia Bor.
0230	Little Ferry Bor.
0231	Lodi Bor.
0232	Lyndhurst Twp.
0233	Mahwah Twp.
0234	Maywood Bor.
0235	Midland Park Bor.
0236	Montvale Bor.
0237	Moonachie Bor.
0238	New Milford Bor.
0239	North Arlington Bor.
0240	Northvale Bor.
0241	Norwood Bor.
0242	Oakland Bor.
0243	Old Tappan Bor.
0244	Oradell Bor.
0245	Palisades Park Bor.
0246	Paramus Bor.
0247	Park Ridge Bor.
0248	Ramsey Bor.
0249	Ridgefield Bor.
0250	Ridgefield Park Village
0251	Ridgewood Village
0252	Riveredge Bor.
0253	Rivervale Twp.
0254	Rochelle Park Twp.
0255	Rockleigh Bor.
0256	Rutherford Bor.
0257	Saddle Brook Twp.

Location Code	Municipality
0258	Saddle River Bor.
0259	South Hackensack Twp.
0260	Teaneck Twp.
0261	Tenafly Bor.
0262	Teterboro Bor.
0263	Upper Saddle River Bor.
0264	Waldwick Bor.
0265	Wallington Bor.
0266	Washington Twp.
0267	Westwood Bor.
0268	Woodcliff Lake Bor.
0269	Wood-Ridge Bor.
0270	Wyckoff Twp.
BURLINGTON COUNTY	
0301	Bass River Twp.
0302	Beverly City
0303	Bordentown City
0304	Bordentown Twp.
0305	Burlington City
0306	Burlington Twp.
0307	Chesterfield Twp.
0308	Cinnaminson Twp.
0309	Delanco Twp.
0310	Delran Twp.
0311	Eastampton Twp.
0312	Edgewater Park Twp.
0313	Evesham Twp.
0314	Fieldsboro Bor.
0315	Florence Twp.
0316	Hainesport Twp.
0317	Lumberton Twp.
0318	Mansfield Twp.
0319	Maple Shade Twp.
0320	Medford Twp.
0321	Medford Lakes Bor.
0322	Moorestown Twp.
0323	Mount Holly Twp.
0324	Mount Laurel Twp.
0325	New Hanover Twp.
0326	No. Hanover Twp.
0327	Palmyra Bor.
0328	Pemberton Bor.
0329	Pemberton Twp.
0330	Riverside Twp.
0331	Riverton Bor.
0332	Shamong Twp.
0333	Southampton Twp.
0334	Springfield Twp.
0335	Tabernacle Twp.
0336	Washington Twp.
0337	Westampton Twp.
0338	Willingboro Twp.
0339	Woodland Twp.
0340	Wrightstown Bor.
CAMDEN COUNTY	
0401	Audubon Bor.
0402	Audubon Park Bor.
0403	Barrington Bor.
0404	Bellmawr Bor.
0405	Berlin Bor.
0406	Berlin Twp.
0407	Brooklawn Bor.
0408	Camden City
0409	Cherry Hill Twp.
0410	Chesilhurst Bor.
0411	Clementon Bor.
0412	Collingswood Bor.
0413	Gibbsboro Bor.
0414	Gloucester City
0415	Gloucester Twp.
0416	Haddon Twp.
0417	Haddonfield Bor.
0418	Haddon Heights Bor.
0419	Hi Nella Bor.
0420	Laurel Springs Bor.
0421	Lawnside Bor.
0422	Lindenwold Bor.
0423	Magnolia Bor.
0424	Merchantville Bor.
0425	Mt. Ephraim Bor.
0426	Oaklyn Bor.

Location Code	Municipality
0427	Pennsauken Twp.
0428	Pine Hill Bor.
0429	Pine Valley Bor.
0430	Runnemede Bor.
0431	Somerdale Bor.
0432	Stratford Bor.
0433	Tavistock Bor.
0434	Voorhees Twp.
0435	Waterford Twp.
0436	Winslow Twp.
0437	Woodlynne Bor.
CAPE MAY COUNTY	
0501	Avalon Bor.
0502	Cape May City
0503	Cape May Point Bor.
0504	Dennis Twp.
0505	Lower Twp.
0506	Middle Twp.
0507	North Wildwood City
0508	Ocean City City
0509	Sea Isle City City
0510	Stone Harbor Bor.
0511	Upper Twp.
0512	West Cape May Bor.
0513	West Wildwood Bor.
0514	Wildwood City
0515	Wildwood Crest Bor.
0516	Woodbine Bor.
CUMBERLAND COUNTY	
0601	Bridgeton City
0602	Commercial Twp.
0603	Deerfield Twp.
0604	Downe Twp.
0605	Fairfield Twp.
0606	Greenwich Twp.
0607	Hopewell Twp.
0608	Lawrence Twp.
0609	Maurice River Twp.
0610	Millville City
0611	Shiloh Bor.
0612	Stow Creek Twp.
0613	Upper Deerfield Twp.
0614	Vineland City
ESSEX COUNTY	
0701	Belleville Twp.
0702	Bloomfield Twp.
0703	Caldwell Borough Twp.
0704	Cedar Grove Twp.
0705	East Orange City
0706	Essex Fells Twp.
0707	Fairfield Twp.
0708	Glen Ridge Twp.
0709	Irvington Twp.
0710	Livingston Twp.
0711	Maplewood Twp.
0712	Millburn Twp.
0713	Montclair Twp.
0714	Newark City
0715	North Caldwell Twp.
0716	Nutley Twp.
0717	Orange City Twp.
0718	Roseland Bor.
0719	South Orange Village
0720	Verona Twp.
0721	West Caldwell Twp.
0722	West Orange Twp.
GLOUCESTER COUNTY	
0801	Clayton Bor.
0802	Deptford Twp.
0803	East Greenwich Twp.
0804	Elk Twp.
0805	Franklin Twp.
0806	Glassboro Bor.
0807	Greenwich Twp.
0808	Harrison Twp.
0809	Logan Twp.
0810	Mantua Twp.
0811	Monroe Twp.
0812	National Park Bor.

Location Code	Municipality
0813	Newfield Bor.
0814	Paulsboro Bor.
0815	Pitman Bor.
0816	South Harrison Twp.
0817	Swedesboro Bor.
0818	Washington Twp.
0819	Wenonah Bor.
0820	West Deptford Twp.
0821	Westville Bor.
0822	Woodbury City
0823	Woodbury Heights Bor.
0824	Woolwich Twp.
HUDSON COUNTY	
0901	Bayonne City
0902	East Newark Bor.
0903	Guttenberg Town
0904	Harrison Town
0905	Hoboken City
0906	Jersey City City
0907	Kearny Town
0908	North Bergen Twp.
0909	Secaucus Town
0910	Union City City
0911	Weehawken Twp.
0912	West New York
HUNTERDON COUNTY	
1001	Alexandria Twp.
1002	Bethlehem Twp.
1003	Bloomsbury Bor.
1004	Califon Bor.
1005	Clinton Town
1006	Clinton Twp.
1007	Delaware Twp.
1008	East Amwell Twp.
1009	Flemington Bor.
1010	Franklin Twp.
1011	Frenchtown Bor.
1012	Glen Gardner Bor.
1013	Hampton Bor.
1014	High Bridge Bor.
1015	Holland Twp.
1016	Kingswood Twp.
1017	Lambertville City
1018	Lebanon Bor.
1019	Lebanon Twp.
1020	Milford Bor.
1021	Raritan Twp.
1022	Readington Twp.
1023	Stockton Bor.
1024	Tewksbury Twp.
1025	Union Twp.
1026	West Amwell Twp.
MERCER COUNTY	
1101	East Windsor Twp.
1102	Ewing Twp.
1103	Hamilton Twp.
1104	Hightstown Bor.
1105	Hopewell Bor.
1106	Hopewell Twp.
1107	Lawrence Twp.
1108	Pennington Bor.
1109	Princeton Bor.
1110	Princeton Twp.
1111	Trenton City
1112	Washington Twp.
1113	West Windsor Twp.
MIDDLESEX COUNTY	
1201	Carteret Bor.
1202	Cranbury Twp.
1203	Dunellen Bor.
1204	East Brunswick
1205	Edison Twp.
1206	Helmetta Bor.
1207	Highland Park Bor.
1208	Jamesburg Bor.
1209	Metuchen Bor.
1210	Middlesex Bor.
1211	Milltown Bor.
1212	Monroe Twp.

INSTRUCTIONS FOR
APPLICATION TO REGISTER A BUSINESS
IN NEW JERSEY
(CONTINUED)

41

TABLE B - NEW JERSEY COUNTY / MUNICIPALITY CODES

Enter the Appropriate Four-Digit Number in the Boxes Provided on Page 17, Item J.

Location Code	Municipality	Location Code	Municipality	Location Code	Municipality	Location Code	Municipality
1213	New Brunswick City	1416	Lincoln Park Bor.	1707	Oldmans Twp.	2103	Belvidere Town
1214	North Brunswick Twp.	1417	Madison Bor.	1708	Penns Grove Bor.	2104	Blairstown Twp.
1215	Old Bridge Twp.	1418	Mendham Bor.	1709	Pennsville Twp.	2105	Franklin Twp.
1216	Perth Amboy City	1419	Mendham Twp.	1710	Pilesgrove Twp.	2106	Frelinghuysen Twp.
1217	Piscataway Twp.	1420	Mine Hill Twp.	1711	Pittsgrove Twp.	2107	Greenwich Twp.
1218	Plainsboro Twp.	1421	Montville Twp.	1712	Quinton Twp.	2108	Hackettstown Town
1219	Sayreville Bor.	1422	Morris Twp.	1713	Salem City	2109	Hardwick Twp.
1220	South Amboy City	1423	Morris Plains Bor.	1714	Upper Pittsgrove Twp.	2110	Harmony Twp.
1221	South Brunswick Twp.	1424	Morristown Town	1715	Woodstown Bor	2111	Hope Twp.
1222	South Plainfield Bor.	1425	Mountain Lakes Bor.			2112	Independence Twp.
1223	South River Bor.	1426	Mount Arlington Bor.	**SOMERSET COUNTY**		2113	Knowlton Twp.
1224	Spotswood Bor.	1427	Mount Olive Twp.	1801	Bedminster Twp.	2114	Liberty Twp.
1225	Woodbridge Twp.	1428	Netcong Bor.	1802	Bernards Twp.	2115	Lopatcong Twp.
		1429	Par-Troy Hills Twp.	1803	Bernardsville Bor.	2116	Mansfield Twp.
MONMOUTH COUNTY		1430	Passaic Twp.	1804	Bound Brook Bor.	2117	Oxford Twp.
1301	Aberdeen Twp.	1431	Pequannock Twp.	1805	Branchburg Twp.	2118	Pahaquarry Twp.
1302	Allenhurst Bor.	1432	Randolph Twp.	1806	Bridgewater Twp.	2119	Phillipsburg Town
1303	Allentown Bor.	1433	Riverdale Bor.	1807	Far Hills Bor.	2120	Pohatcong Twp.
1304	Asbury Park City	1434	Rockaway Bor.	1808	Franklin Twp.	2121	Washington Bor.
1305	Atlantic Highlands Bor.	1435	Rockaway Twp.	1809	Green Brook Twp.	2122	Washington Twp.
1306	Avon-by-the-sea Bor.	1436	Roxbury Twp.	1810	Hillsborough Twp.	2123	White Twp.
1307	Belmar Bor.	1437	Victory Gardens Bor.	1811	Manville Bor.		
1308	Bradley Beach Bor.	1438	Washington Twp.	1812	Millstone Bor.	2200	ALABAMA
1309	Brielle Bor.	1439	Wharton Bor.	1813	Montgomery Twp.	2300	ALASKA
1310	Colts Neck Twp.			1814	North Plainfield Bor.	2400	ARIZONA
1311	Deal Bor.	**OCEAN COUNTY**		1815	Peapack-Gladstone Bor.	2500	ARKANSAS
1312	Eatontown Bor.	1501	Barnegat Twp.	1816	Raritan Bor.	2600	CALIFORNIA
1313	Englishtown Bor.	1502	Barnegat Light Bor.	1817	Rocky Hill Bor.	2700	COLORADO
1314	Fair Haven Bor.	1503	Bay Head Bor.	1818	Somerville Bor.	2800	CONNECTICUT
1315	Farmingdale	1504	Beach Haven Bor.	1819	South Bound Brook Bor.	2900	DELAWARE
1316	Freehold Bor.	1505	Beachwood Bor.	1820	Warren Twp.	3000	DISTRICT OF COLUMBIA
1317	Freehold Twp.	1506	Berkeley Twp.	1821	Watchung Bor.	3100	FLORIDA
1318	Hazlet Twp.	1507	Brick Twp.			3200	GEORGIA
1319	Highlands Bor.	1508	Dover Twp.	**SUSSEX COUNTY**		3300	HAWAII
1320	Holmdel Twp.	1509	Eagleswood Twp.	1901	Andover Bor.	3400	IDAHO
1321	Howell Twp.	1510	Harvey Cedars Bor.	1902	Andover Twp.	3500	ILLINOIS
1322	Interlaken Bor.	1511	Island Heights Bor.	1903	Branchville Bor.	3600	INDIANA
1323	Keansburg Bor.	1512	Jackson Twp.	1904	Byram Twp.	3700	IOWA
1324	Keyport Bor.	1513	Lacey Twp.	1905	Frankford Twp.	3800	KANSAS
1325	Little Silver Bor.	1514	Lakehurst Bor.	1906	Franklin Bor.	3900	KENTUCKY
1326	Loch Arbour Village	1515	Lakewood Twp.	1907	Fredon Twp.	4000	LOUISIANA
1327	Long Branch City	1516	Lavallette Bor.	1908	Green Twp.	4100	MAINE
1328	Manalapan Twp.	1517	Little Egg Harbor Twp.	1909	Hamburg Bor.	4200	MARYLAND
1329	Manasquan Bor.	1518	Long Beach Twp.	1910	Hampton Twp.	4300	MASSACHUSETTS
1330	Marlboro Twp.	1519	Manchester Twp.	1911	Hardystown Twp.	4400	MICHIGAN
1331	Matawan Bor.	1520	Mantoloking Bor.	1912	Hopatcong Bor.	4500	MINNESOTA
1332	Middletown Twp.	1521	Ocean Twp.	1913	Lafayette Twp.	4600	MISSISSIPPI
1333	Millstone Twp.	1522	Ocean Gate Bor.	1914	Montague Twp.	4700	MISSOURI
1334	Monmouth Beach Bor.	1523	Pine Beach Bor.	1915	Newton Town	4800	MONTANA
1335	Neptune Twp.	1524	Plumsted Twp.	1916	Ogdensburg Bor.	4900	NEBRASKA
1336	Neptune City Bor.	1525	Pt. Pleasant Bor.	1917	Sandyston Twp.	5000	NEVADA
1337	Ocean Twp.	1526	Pt. Pleasant Beach Bor.	1918	Sparta Twp.	5100	NEW HAMPSHIRE
1338	Oceanport Bor.	1527	Seaside Heights Bor.	1919	Stanhope Bor.	5200	NEW JERSEY
1339	Red Bank Bor.	1528	Seaside Park Bor.	1920	Stillwater Twp.	5300	NEW MEXICO
1340	Roosevelt Bor.	1529	Ship Bottom Bor.	1921	Sussex Bor.	5400	NEW YORK
1341	Rumson Bor.	1530	South Toms River Bor.	1922	Vernon Twp.	5500	NORTH CAROLINA
1342	Sea Bright Bor.	1531	Stafford Twp.	1923	Walpack Twp.	5600	NORTH DAKOTA
1343	Sea Girt Bor.	1532	Surf City Bor.	1924	Wantage Twp.	5700	OHIO
1344	Shrewsbury Bor.	1533	Tuckerton Bor.			5800	OKLAHOMA
1345	Shrewsbury Twp.			**UNION COUNTY**		5900	OREGON
1346	South Belmar Bor.	**PASSAIC COUNTY**		2001	Berkeley Heights Twp.	6000	PENNSYLVANIA
1347	Spring Lake Bor.	1601	Bloomingdale Bor.	2002	Clark Twp.	6100	RHODE ISLAND
1348	Spring Lake Heights Bor.	1602	Clifton City	2003	Cranford Twp.	6200	SOUTH CAROLINA
1349	Tinton Falls Bor.	1603	Haledon Bor.	2004	Elizabeth City	6300	SOUTH DAKOTA
1350	Union Beach Bor.	1604	Hawthorne Bor.	2005	Fanwood Bor.	6400	TENNESSEE
1351	Upper Freehold Twp.	1605	Little Falls Twp.	2006	Garwood Bor.	6500	TEXAS
1352	Wall Twp.	1606	North Haledon Bor.	2007	Hillside Twp.	6600	UTAH
1353	West Long Branch Bor.	1607	Passaic City	2008	Kenilworth Bor.	6700	VERMONT
		1608	Paterson City	2009	Linden City	6800	VIRGINIA
MORRIS COUNTY		1609	Pompton Lakes Bor.	2010	Mountainside Bor.	6900	WASHINGTON
1401	Boonton Town	1610	Prospect Park Bor.	2011	New Providence Bor.	7000	WEST VIRGINIA
1402	Boonton Twp.	1611	Ringwood Bor.	2012	Plainfield City	7100	WISCONSIN
1403	Butler Bor.	1612	Totowa Bor.	2013	Rahway City	7200	WYOMING
1404	Chatham Bor.	1613	Wanaque Bor.	2014	Roselle Bor.	7300	PUERTO RICO
1405	Chatham Twp.	1614	Wayne Twp.	2015	Roselle Park Bor.	7400	NETHERLANDS
1406	Chester Bor.	1615	West Milford Twp.	2016	Scotch Plains	7500	BELGIUM
1407	Chester Twp.	1616	West Paterson Bor.	2017	Springfield Twp.	7600	ARGENTINA
1408	Denville Twp.			2018	Summit City	7700	CANADA
1409	Dover Twp.	**SALEM COUNTY**		2019	Union Twp.	7800	MEXICO
1410	East Hanover Twp.	1701	Alloway Twp.	2020	Westfield Town	7900	VIRGIN ISLANDS
1411	Florham Park Bor.	1702	Carneys Point Twp.	2021	Winfield Twp.	8000	ENGLAND
1312	Hanover Twp.	1703	Elmer Bor.			8100	CHINA
1413	Harding Twp.	1704	Elsinboro Twp.	**WARREN COUNTY**		8200	GERMANY
1414	Jefferson Twp.	1705	Lower Alloways Creek Twp.	2101	Allamuchy Twp.	8300	IRELAND
1415	Kinnelon Bor.	1706	Mannington Twp.	2102	Alpha Bor.	8400	GREECE
						8500	ISRAEL

- 13 -

INSTRUCTIONS FOR
APPLICATION TO REGISTER A BUSINESS
IN NEW JERSEY
(CONTINUED)

DIVISION OF TAXATION
District Offices

Offices for Taxpayers Assistance and Forms

TRENTON – Taxation Building
50 Barrack St. – 1st Floor Lobby
Box CN 269
Trenton, NJ 08646
(609) 292-6400
Toll Free: (800) 323-4400

REGIONAL OFFICES:

NEPTUNE

1828 West Lake Avenue, 3rd Floor
Neptune, NJ 07753

CAMDEN

One Port Center, Suite 200
Camden, NJ 08103

FAIR LAWN

2208 Route 208, South
Fair Lawn, NJ 07410
(201) 791-0500

NEWARK

124 Halsey Street, 2nd Floor
Newark, NJ 07101
(973) 648-2567

NORTHFIELD

1915-A New Road, Rt. 9
Northfield, NJ 08225
(609) 645-6673

QUAKERBRIDGE

NO WALK-IN ASSISTANCE
Conference and Appeals Branch
Quakerbridge Plaza Office Complex
Bldg. 5 - 3rd Floor Quakerbridge
Mercerville, NJ 08619

SOMERVILLE

75 Veterans Memorial Dr. East
Suite 103
Somerville, NJ 08876

You may also register your business online by going to the NJ web site at:
http://www.state.nj.us/treasury/revenue/dcr/reg/sos_dcrnew01.prod.htm

Hours of operation 8:30 a.m. to 4:30 p.m. Monday through Friday.

NEW JERSEY WEB SITE

WWW.NJ.GOV/NJBUSINESS/ or WWW.STATE.NJ.US

NEW JERSEY HOTLINES

Personal Income Tax .... (609) 633-6657

Business Tax .... (609) 633-6900

7
RECORD KEEPING FOR THE NEW JERSEY SALES TAX BUREAU

In a prior chapter we discussed the type of bookkeeping system you might maintain for your business. If you adhere to these suggestions, save all your receipts, and report your income/expenses properly, you'll be in good shape for most IRS audits. Unfortunately, the State of New Jersey Sales Tax Bureau conducts a different type of audit. They are interested in your payment of sales tax. The State of New Jersey may also conduct an audit of income and expenses in addition to the audit for sales tax.

In New Jersey, many items are subject to the 6.875% sales tax. This means that you as a business owner would collect the sales tax and every month or quarter remit what you have collected to the New Jersey Sales Tax Bureau.

If you sell taxable items or provide taxable services in New Jersey, you are required to collect 6.875% sales tax and remit it to the State. You must file a New Jersey Sales and Use Tax Quarterly Return ST-50 every three months, even if in that particular quarter you collected no tax. Businesses that collect more than $500 per month in sales tax must also file the monthly remittance statements ST-51. As of January 1, 2005, all sales tax submissions must be made on-line or by phone.

What actually happens in a sales tax audit is that the State requires the business to prove why they did not send in sales tax on certain items. As an example, many retailers and wholesalers sell taxable and non-taxable items. When the business owner submits his quarterly sales tax form, he shows the taxable and non-taxable sales. The State may actually come in and ask you to prove why you did not collect and remit sales tax on certain goods.

NJ Division of Taxation
Sales and Use Tax Quarterly Return Confirmation

ST-50

FEIN: 205-222-222/000	**Quarter/Yr:** 4/2016
Business Name: JAMY'S DONUT SHOPPE	
Quarter Ending Date: 12/31/2016	**Return Due Date:** 1/20/2017
Date Filed: 12/31/2016	

Your Return Has Been Submitted To The Division.

Contact Name: JON CARLIN
Telephone Number:
Extension:
E-mail Address: joncarlin@yahoo.com
Confirmation Number: 123456789

1. **Gross Receipts for Quarter** (To Nearest Dollar)	$18,500
2. **Deductions** (To Nearest Dollar)	$ 6,071
3. **Balance Subject to Tax** (Line 1 minus Line 2)	$12,429
4. **Sales Tax Due** (Greater of amount collected or applicable rate of Line 3)	$ 855
5. **Use Tax Due**	$ 0
6. **Total Tax Due** (Line 4 plus Line 5)	$ 855
7. **Total Payments Made**	$ 500
8. **Quarterly Amount Due** (Line 6 minus Line 7)	$ 355
9. **Penalty and Interest**	$ 0
10. **Adjusted Amount Due** (Line 8 plus Line 9)	$ 355

Print   Close Window

N.J. QUARTERLY ON-LINE REPORTING FORM

Each Question Must Be Answered Completely

11. a. Will you collect New Jersey Sales Tax and/or pay Use Tax? .... ☒ Yes ☐ No
    GIVE EXACT DATE YOU EXPECT TO MAKE FIRST SALE __1__ / __1__ / __17__
                                   Month   Day   Year

    b. Will you need to make exempt purchases for your inventory or to produce your product? .... ☒ Yes ☐ No

    c. Is your business located in (check applicable box(es)): ☐ Atlantic City ☐ Salem County
                                                 ☐ North Wildwood ☐ Wildwood Crest ☐ Wildwood
    d. Do you have more than one location in New Jersey that collects New Jersey Sales Tax? (If yes, see instructions) ...... ☐ Yes ☒ No

    e. Do you, in the regular course of business, sell, store, deliver or transport natural gas or electricity to users or customers
    in this state whether by mains, lines or pipes located within this State or by any other means of delivery? .... ☐ Yes ☒ No

12. Do you intend to sell cigarettes? .... ☐ Yes ☒ No
    Note: If yes, complete the REG-L form on page 45 in this booklet and return with your completed NJ-REG.
    To obtain a cigarette retail or vending machine license complete the form CM-100 on page 47.
13. a. Are you a **distributor** or **wholesaler** of tobacco products other than cigarettes? .... ☐ Yes ☒ No

    b. Do you purchase tobacco products other than cigarettes from outside the State of New Jersey? .... ☐ Yes ☒ No

14. Are you a manufacturer, wholesaler, distributor or retailer of "litter-generating products"? See instructions for retailer ...... ☐ Yes ☒ No
    liability and definition of litter-generating products.
15. Are you an owner or operator of a sanitary landfill facility in New Jersey? .... ☐ Yes ☒ No
    IF YES, indicate D.E.P. Facility # and type (See instructions) _____
16. a. Do you operate a facility that has the total combined capacity to store 200,000 gallons or more of petroleum products? .. ☐ Yes ☒ No

    b. Do you operate a facility that has the total combined capacity to store 20,000 gallons
    (equals 167,043 pounds) of hazardous chemicals? .... ☐ Yes ☒ No

    c. Do you store petroleum products or hazardous chemicals at a public storage terminal? .... ☐ Yes ☒ No
    Name of terminal _____

17. a. Will you be involved with the sale or transport of motor fuels and/or petroleum? .... ☐ Yes ☒ No
    Note: If yes, complete the REG-L form in this booklet and return with your completed NJ-REG.
    To obtain a motor fuels retail or transport license complete and return the CM-100 in this booklet.

    b. Will your company be engaged in the refining and/or distributing of petroleum products for distribution in this State or
    the importing of petroleum products into New Jersey for consumption in New Jersey? .... ☐ Yes ☒ No

    c. Will your business activity require you to issue a Direct Payment Permit in lieu of payment of the Petroleum Products
    Gross Receipts Tax on your purchases of petroleum products? .... ☐ Yes ☒ No
18. Will you be providing goods and services as a direct contractor or subcontractor to the state, other public agencies
    including local governments, colleges and universities and school boards, or to casino licensees? .... ☐ Yes ☒ No
19. Will you be engaged in the business of renting motor vehicles for the transportation of persons
    or non-commercial freight? .... ☐ Yes ☒ No

20. Is your business a hotel, motel, bed & breakfast or similar facility and located in the State of New Jersey? .... ☐ Yes ☒ No
21. Do you hold a permit or license, issued by the New Jersey Department of Transportation, to erect and maintain
    an outdoor advertising sign or to engage in the business of outdoor advertising? .. Fee expired effective 7/1/07 ....

22. Do you make retail sales of new motor vehicle tires, or sell or lease motor vehicles? .... ☐ Yes ☒ No

23. Do you provide "cosmetic medical procedures" or goods or occupancies directly associated with such procedures? .... ☐ Yes ☒ No
    (See description of Cosmetic Procedures Gross Receipts Tax in the list of Taxes of the State of New Jersey, page 5.)
    Type of Business _____
24. Do you sell voice grade access telecommunications or mobile telecommunications to a customer with a primary
    place of use in this State? .... ☐ Yes ☒ No

25. Will you make retail sales of "fur clothing"? .... ☐ Yes ☒ No
    (See full description of Fur Clothing Retail Gross Receipts Tax in the list of Taxes of the State of New Jersey, page 5)

26. Contact Information: Person AMY CARLIN _____ Title: PARTNER _____
    Daytime Phone: (908) 555 - 2738 ____ Ext. _____ E-mail address: ACARLIN@YAHOO.COM ____

    Signature of Owner, Partner or Officer: _____

    Title PARTNER _____ Date: 2/1/17 ____

NO FEE IS REQUIRED TO FILE THIS FORM

IF YOU ARE A SOLE PROPRIETOR OR A PARTNERSHIP WITHOUT EMPLOYEES - **STOP HERE** -
IF YOU HAVE EMPLOYEES PROCEED TO THE STATE OF NJ NEW HIRE REPORTING FORM ON PAGE 29

IF YOU ARE FORMING A CORPORATION, LIMITED LIABILITY COMPANY, LIMITED PARTNERSHIP, OR A LIMITED
LIABILITY PARTNERSHIP YOU MUST CONTINUE ANSWERING APPLICABLE QUESTIONS ON PAGES 23 AND 24

SALES AND USE TAX INSTRUCTIONS

New Jersey Sales and Use Tax EZ Telefile System Instructions
(Forms ST-50 Quarterly Return and ST-51 Monthly Remittance Statement)
Do NOT Use for 3rd Quarter 2006

Rate Change

The New Jersey Sales and Use Tax will be reduced in two phases between 2017 and 2018. P.L. 2016, c.57 decreases the Sales and Use Tax rate from 7% to 6.875% on and after January 1, 2017. The tax rate will decrease to 6.625% on and after January 1, 2018.

Filing Forms ST-50/51 by Phone

Complete the EZ Telefile Worksheet, call the Business Paperless Telefiling System at 609-341-4800, and select "1" from the menu for the Sales and Use Tax EZ File System. You will be prompted to enter the information from your worksheet on your touch-tone telephone keypad. (NOTE: For best results, do not use a phone such as a cordless or cellular phone that has a keypad in the handset.) The system provides step-by-step instructions and repeats your entries to ensure accuracy. When your return is accepted, you will be given a seven-digit confirmation number as proof that your return was successfully filed. The telefiling system is available 24 hours a day, seven days a week.

Payments. The system automatically calculates the total amount that you owe based on the information that you provide. Be sure to enter all of the information that is requested on the worksheet. (See "Instructions for Telefile Worksheet" on page 3.) Payments must be made electronically using either electronic check (e-check), electronic funds transfer (EFT), or credit card. (See "How to Pay" on page 2.) During your phone call you will have an opportunity to pay the amount due by e-check or EFT debit. You can also pay the amount due outside the telefiling system using a credit card or EFT (debit or credit).

Identification. You will be asked to enter your New Jersey Taxpayer Identification Number and either your 4-digit Sales Tax Personal Identification Number (PIN) or the first four characters of your registered taxpayer name to access the system.

NOTE: For filing periods beginning on and after February 1, 2016, if your business sells new or used boats or other vessels (including motorboats, sailboats, yachts, and cruisers) that are eligible for the partial Sales and Use Tax exemption (half of the applicable Sales Tax rate) and the $20,000 Sales Tax cap, you cannot use the Sales and Use Tax EZ Telefile System. You must file all quarterly returns and monthly remittance statements online and make the required payments electronically, even if your business made no sales that were eligible for the reduced Sales Tax rate or the Sales Tax cap for a particular period.

More information on the partial Sales Tax exemption and the $20,000 Sales Tax cap is available on the Division of Taxation's website at www.state.nj.us/treasury/taxation/boatbill.shtml.

Filing Online

You can also file your Sales and Use Tax Returns and Remittance Statements (Forms ST-50/51) online at the Division of Taxation's website (www.njtaxation.org). Choose the "Businesses" tab in the center column, select "File Business Taxes/Fees," and then choose "Sales and Use Tax" to access the link to the online filing application.

Other Sales and Use Tax Returns

The forms listed below cannot be filed through the Sales and Use Tax EZ File System. Taxpayers must continue to complete and file these forms on paper according to the instructions that accompany the forms.

- Annual Business Use Tax Return (Form ST-18B).
- Sales and Use Tax Energy Return (Form ST-EN).

Who Must File

Every entity registered in New Jersey to collect Sales Tax or to remit Use Tax must file Sales and Use Tax returns and remittance statements on a regular basis. The amount of tax due for each filing period must be remitted to the State on or before the due date of the filing.

- **Quarterly Return (ST-50)** – All businesses are required to file Form ST-50 for each quarter, even if no tax is due and/or no sales were made for that particular quarter. The quarterly return must show total gross receipts for the entire three-month period covered by that quarterly return. The quarterly payment does not have to be made at the same time the ST-50 return is filed; however, making only the quarterly payment does not satisfy the requirement to file the return.

- **Monthly Remittance Statement (ST-51)** – Businesses that collected more than $30,000 in New Jersey Sales and Use Tax during the preceding calendar year must also file Form ST-51 for the first and/or second month of a calendar quarter and make the required payment if the amount of tax due for that month exceeds $500. If $30,000 or less in Sales and Use Tax was collected in New Jersey during the preceding calendar year, a monthly remittance is not required, regardless of the amount of tax due for that particular month. When the amount due for any period covered by Form ST-51 is $500 or less, payment for that month may be remitted with the next quarterly return (Form ST-50). Because no taxpayers are required to file Form ST-51 for periods in which $500 or less is due, there is no provision for a "zero" monthly filing.

Taxpayers that are registered to remit payments by electronic funds transfer (EFT) must make monthly payments of Sales and Use Tax as required and must file ST-50 quarterly returns. EFT payers are not required to file ST-51 monthly remittance statements.

This packet contains four EZ Telefile Worksheets — one for each calendar quarter. You will record both your monthly (if required) and quarterly information on the same worksheet. The EZ Telefile Worksheets may be reproduced for future use. Copies are also available online or by phone. (See "Where to Get Information" on page 5.)

When to File

Both monthly remittance statements and quarterly returns are due by the 20th day of the month following the period covered by the filing. For example, a monthly remittance statement

INSTRUCTIONS FOR FILING THE
NJ SALES TAX RETURNS

(Form ST-51) for the month of November must be filed no later than December 20, and a quarterly return (Form ST-50) for the fourth quarter (ending December 31) must be filed by January 20. If a due date falls on a Saturday, Sunday, or legal holiday, the filing is due on the next business day. Returns and remittance statements transmitted by 11:59 p.m. on the due date will be deemed timely.

How to Pay
Payments made by 11:59 p.m. on the due date will be deemed timely, even if the settlement date (date payment is debited from the account) is after the filing deadline, provided the payment is made by e-check or EFT debit through the Business Paperless Telefiling System, or by credit card.

NOTE: E-check or EFT (debit or credit) payments made using an account that is funded from a financial institution outside the United States will not be accepted.

Electronic Check (e-check)
You will be given an opportunity during your telephone call to pay your tax liability by e-check. If you choose to pay by e-check, be sure to enter the nine-digit routing number and the account number (up to 17 characters – numbers only) in the Payment Information section of the worksheet **before** you make your call.

If you choose not to pay the tax due when you file your quarterly return, you can make an e-check payment by itself in a separate call later. However, your quarterly payment must be made by the due date to avoid penalty and interest charges.

Electronic Funds Transfer (EFT)
Taxpayers with a prior year liability of $10,000 or more in any tax are required to make their payments for all taxes by EFT. Other taxpayers may voluntarily submit payments by EFT with the approval of the Division of Revenue and Enterprise Services. You must enroll with the Division of Revenue and Enterprise Services to pay by either EFT debit or credit. The enrollment process may take several weeks. For more information on making payments by EFT debit or credit, call 609-292-9292, write to New Jersey Division of Revenue and Enterprise Services, EFT Unit, PO Box 191, Trenton, NJ 08646-0191, or visit the Division of Revenue and Enterprise Services' website at www.state. nj.us/treasury/revenue/eft1.shtml. Taxpayers that are required to remit payments by EFT can satisfy the EFT requirement by making e-check or credit card payments. FED Wires or other wire transfers are not acceptable methods of EFT payments.

If you are an EFT debit payer, you can initiate payments through the Business Paperless Telefiling System when filing. If you choose not to pay the tax due at the same time you file your quarterly return, you can make an EFT debit payment by itself in a separate call later. EFT credit payers must make their Sales and Use Tax payments as separate transactions outside the Business Paperless Telefiling System. Your payment must be made by the due date to avoid penalty and interest charges.

Credit Card
To pay your tax liability by credit card, call 888-673-7694 or go to the Division of Taxation's website at www.njtaxation.org after you have completed your telephone filing and received a confirmation number. When paying online, choose the "Businesses" tab in the center column and then choose "File

Business Taxes/Fees." Select "Sales and Use Tax" and then click on the link "File Online ST-50/51." Once you have entered your New Jersey Taxpayer Identification Number and PIN (or business name), choose "All Other Payments – Deficiencies" from the list, enter the month and year for which you are making a payment, and continue. Fees apply when you pay by credit card. The fee is added to your actual payment.

Penalties, Interest, and Fees
Failure to file a return by the due date and/or failure to remit any taxes due by the due date will result in penalty and interest charges. Anyone required to collect Sales and Use Tax does so as a trustee on behalf of the State of New Jersey. As trustees of the State, business owners, partners, corporate officers, and some employees of such businesses may be held personally liable for failure to collect the tax when required or for failure to file returns and remit any taxes due on a timely basis.

Late Filing Penalties
The late filing penalty is 5% per month (or fraction thereof) of the balance of tax liability due at original return due date not to exceed 25% of such tax liability. A penalty of $100 per month (or fraction thereof) for each month the return is late will also be imposed.

Late Payment Penalty
The late payment penalty is 5% of the balance of the taxes due and paid late.

Interest
The annual interest rate is 3% above the average predominant prime rate. Interest is imposed each month (or fraction thereof) on the unpaid balance of the tax from the original due date to the date of payment. At the end of each calendar year any tax, penalties, and interest remaining due will become part of the balance on which interest is charged.

NOTE: The average predominant prime rate is the rate as determined by the Board of Governors of the Federal Reserve System, quoted by commercial banks to large businesses on December 1 of the calendar year immediately preceding the calendar year in which the payment was due or as determined by the Director in accordance with N.J.S.A. 54:48-2.

Collection Fees
In addition to the above penalties and interest, if your tax bill is sent to a collection agency, a referral cost recovery fee of 10.7% of the tax due will be added to your liability. If a certificate of debt is issued for your outstanding liability, a fee for the cost of collection may also be imposed.

General Information
Lease Transactions
A lessor must collect Sales Tax from a lessee (person who leases or rents property) on a lease or rental. For transactions with a term of six months or less, Sales Tax must be collected with each periodic payment. For transactions with a duration of more than six months, the tax due on the full term of the lease must be remitted with the monthly remittance statement or quarterly return for the period in which the property was delivered to the lessee. The amount upon which the tax was calculated must be included in gross receipts on the quarterly return (ST-50). This amount will be either the original purchase price of the property or the total of the lease payments.

SALES TAX RETURN
Instructions (Cont.)

Gross Receipts

The accrual method of accounting must be used when reporting gross receipts. Under this method, all receipts are reported in the period in which the sale took place, no matter when, or if, payment is actually received from the customer.

Report gross receipts from all transactions, *including exempt transactions*, that occurred during the three-month reporting period covered by the quarterly return (Form ST-50). This includes, but is not limited to:

- Sales of tangible personal property or digital property, including the rental, storage, and use of tangible personal property or digital property.
- Receipts from parking, garaging, and storing of motor vehicles.
- Receipts from membership fees, initiation fees, and dues.
- Receipts from lease transactions.
- Sales of services.
- Sales of prepared foods.
- Room occupancy charges.
- Admission and amusement charges.
- Receipts from sales of less than $0.08.
- Installment sales or other sales on credit made during the quarter.

NOTE: Businesses subject to Atlantic City Luxury Tax must include in gross receipts the "Total Gross Receipts" amounts reported on Line 1, Column B of Form ST-250 (Combined Atlantic City Luxury Tax/State Sales Tax Monthly Return) for each month of the quarter.

Do not include in gross receipts:

- Installment *payments* from installment sales or other sales on credit.
- Sales Tax collected.
- Trade-in allowances.
- Sales of alcoholic beverages at wholesale.

Adequate records should be maintained showing separately all exclusions from gross receipts.

Deductions

You may deduct the amount of all sales included in gross receipts that are not taxable under New Jersey law. **No deduction may be taken for any amount that was not included in gross receipts on your return.** Deductions may be taken only *once*. For example, if a deduction has been taken for an exempt clothing sale, you may not deduct the amount again as a sale of property that was delivered out of State. Examples of exclusions and deductions include, but are not limited to:

Sales Jointly Taxable by Atlantic City and New Jersey. Businesses subject to Atlantic City Luxury Tax may deduct the "Taxable Receipts" amount from Line 3, Column B of the Combined Atlantic City Luxury Tax/State Sales Tax Monthly Return, Form ST-250.

Excluded Fees for Parking, Garaging, and Storing of Motor Vehicles. Deduct charges for residential parking or employee parking provided by an employer.

Exempt Sales of Tangible Personal Property. Deduct the sales of any tangible personal property that is specifically

exempt from Sales Tax (e.g., sales of grocery foods, clothing, etc.).

Exempt Sales of Services. Deduct total charges for services that are not subject to Sales Tax (e.g., professional services, certain personal services, etc.).

Exempt Occupancies. Deduct receipts from occupancies exceeding 90 consecutive days.

Exempt Admissions. Deduct any admission charges to sporting activities where a patron was a participant.

Sales Covered by Certificates. Deduct receipts from sales of property or services for which a valid New Jersey exemption certificate or Streamlined Sales and Use Tax Agreement Certificate of Exemption was accepted in lieu of tax.

Returned Property. Deduct the total sales price of taxable purchases returned by the customer. Include only the amounts refunded or credited to the customer. Do not include:

- Sales Tax collected on returned purchases.
- Returns that were not subject to Sales Tax.
- Amounts not included in gross receipts on any return.

No deduction may be taken for returned property that has been or will be deducted as an exempt sale on any Sales and Use Tax return.

Property Delivered Out of New Jersey. Deduct total sales of property that was shipped to an out-of-State purchaser by common carrier, delivered to an out-of-State purchaser by the seller in its own carrier, or delivered by the seller to an out-of-State purchaser through an unregulated carrier hired by the seller. Do not include sales of property to an out-of-State purchaser if the customer took possession of the items in New Jersey.

Services Performed Outside of New Jersey. Deduct receipts from services performed outside of New Jersey.

Exempt Capital Improvements. Contractors may deduct sales of services that result in exempt capital improvements to real property. Contractors are required to obtain a fully completed Certificate of Exempt Capital Improvement (Form ST-8) from customers for such transactions.

Rounding Off to Whole Dollars

Eliminate any amount under 50 cents and increase any amount 50 cents or over to the next higher dollar. Round amounts for the quarterly gross receipts and deductions lines only. No other lines are to be rounded.

Instructions for Telefile Worksheet
Identification

New Jersey Taxpayer Identification Number. Enter your 12-digit New Jersey Taxpayer Identification Number as it appears on your New Jersey Certificate of Authority. If your ID number begins with the letters "NJ," enter "6," "5," and the remaining 10 digits. (NOTE: If you do not enter your ID number correctly, you will not be able to file.)

PIN/Taxpayer Name. Enter your four-digit Sales Tax PIN (Personal Identification Number) or the first four characters of your registered taxpayer name. If you are entering your taxpayer name, use only letters and numbers. Omit symbols and spaces.

SALES TAX RETURN
Instructions (Cont.)

(NOTE: If you do not enter your PIN or the first four characters of your taxpayer name correctly, you will not be able to file.)

Contact Phone Number. Enter the area code and phone number of a contact person for the taxpayer.

Tax Preparer's Identification Number. If the return or remittance statement is being filed by a tax preparer, enter the preparer's nine-digit federal identification number or Social Security number. This information will be requested during the signature portion of the phone call.

Return Information

FORM ST-51 – MONTHLY REMITTANCE STATEMENT
Complete this section if you are filing a monthly remittance statement for the first or second month of the quarter. *You are required to file a monthly remittance statement only if you collected more than $30,000 in Sales and Use Tax in New Jersey during the preceding calendar year, and only if the amount of tax due for that month exceeds $500.* If you are filing a quarterly return, go to "Form ST-50 — Quarterly Return," below.

There are two monthly remittance statement sections on the worksheet; one for the first month of the quarter and one for the second month of the quarter. Complete the section that corresponds to the month for which you are filing.

Line 1 – Period Covered by Remittance Statement. The two-digit number of the month (e.g., "01" for January, "02" for February) covered by the remittance statement is preprinted on this line of your worksheet. Enter the four-digit year in which the month fell in the boxes to the right of the month.

Line 2 – Amount of Tax Due. Multiply the total monthly taxable receipts (gross receipts minus deductions) by the Sales Tax rate. Do not include in gross receipts amounts collected for Sales Tax. Enter on Line 2 the larger of this figure or the actual amount of Sales Tax collected for that month. Also include any Use Tax that is due. NOTE: A monthly remittance statement cannot be filed by phone if the amount due is less than one dollar. Monthly payments of less than one dollar must be included with your quarterly return.

Line 3 – Penalty and Interest. Calculate any penalty and interest charges incurred for late payment and/or late filing for the month and enter the amount on Line 3. If you are unable to determine this amount, enter "0." The State will calculate the penalties and interest and send you a bill.

Line 4 – Total Amount Due. The system will calculate the total amount due and provide the amount to you. Enter the amount stated on Line 4. Continue completing the worksheet with the "Payment Information" section. (See instructions on page 5.)

FORM ST-50 – QUARTERLY RETURN
Complete this section when you are filing for the third month of the quarter. A quarterly return must be filed for each quarter, even if no tax is due and/or no sales were made during that quarter.

Line 1 – Period Covered by Return. The number that reflects the calendar quarter covered by the return (e.g., "1" for the first quarter, "2" for the second quarter, etc.) is preprinted on this line of your worksheet. Enter the four-digit year in which the quarter fell in the boxes to the right of the quarter.

Line 2 – Gross Receipts for Quarter. Enter on Line 2 the total gross receipts (to the nearest dollar) from all transactions, including exempt transactions, that occurred during the three-month reporting period covered by the return. (See "Gross Receipts" on page 3 for more information.) If you had no gross receipts for the quarter, enter "0."

Line 3 – Deductions. Enter on Line 3 the amount of all sales (to the nearest dollar) included on Line 2 that are not taxable under New Jersey law. (See "Deductions" on page 3 for more information.) If you had no deductions for the quarter, enter "0."

Line 4 – Amount of Tax Collected. Enter on Line 4 the amount of Sales Tax collected for the quarter. If you did not collect any Sales Tax for the quarter, enter "0."

Line 5 – Sales Tax Due. The system will calculate the Sales Tax due and provide the amount to you. (The amount of Sales Tax due may be greater than the amount collected.) Enter the amount stated on Line 5.

Line 6 – Use Tax Due. Enter on Line 6 the total amount of Use Tax due for taxable tangible personal property or taxable services used during the quarter on which no Sales Tax was paid. (For more information, see publication ANJ-7, *Use Tax in New Jersey.*)

Do not include here any tax due on lease transactions. If you had no Use Tax liability for the quarter, enter "0."

NOTE: Direct payment permit holders enter the total Sales and Use Tax liability on taxable purchases and uses during the quarter covered by the return.

Line 7 – Total Tax Due. The system will calculate the total tax due and provide the amount to you. Enter the amount stated on Line 7.

Line 8 – Total Monthly Payments Previously Made. If you have already paid part of your quarterly liability with a monthly remittance statement (Form ST-51) for the first and/or second month of the quarter, or by electronic funds transfer, enter the total of these payments on Line 8. If you did not make any monthly payments for the quarter, enter "0."

Line 9 – Quarterly Amount Due. The system will calculate the Sales and Use Tax balance due for the quarter and provide the amount to you. Enter the amount stated on Line 9. If your total monthly payments (Line 8) exceed the total tax due (Line 7), you may be eligible for a refund. (To obtain a refund you must file a Claim for Refund, Form A-3730, which is available online and by phone. See "Where to Get Information" on page 5.) Enter "0" here and on Line 11 and continue filing the quarterly return.

Line 10 – Penalty and Interest. Calculate any penalty and interest charges incurred for late payment and/or late filing for the quarter and enter the amount on Line 10. If you are unable to determine this amount, enter "0." You will be billed for any penalty or interest due.

Line 11 – Total Amount Due. The system will calculate the total amount due for the quarter and provide the amount to you. Enter the amount stated on Line 11. If you have a balance due, you must pay by e-check, credit card, or EFT. (See "How to Pay" on page 2.) You are not required to submit your payment on the same date as your telephone call, however, your payment must be made by the due date to avoid penalty and interest charges.

SALES TAX RETURN
Instructions (Cont.)

Payment Information

If you want to pay by e-check, enter on the worksheet the nine-digit bank routing number, the account number (omit hyphens, spaces, symbols, and letters), the type of account, and the date you want the payment to be debited from your account. If you are paying by EFT debit during your phone call, enter only the account type and the payment debit date. The earliest date you may select is the next business day. However, payment transactions initiated by 11:59 p.m. on the due date will be deemed timely, even if the settlement date (date payment is debited from the account) is after the filing deadline.

You can also pay by credit card or EFT (debit or credit) after you have completed your telephone filing and received a confirmation number. (See "How to Pay" on page 2.)

NOTE: E-check or EFT (debit or credit) payments made using an account that is funded from a financial institution outside the United States will not be accepted.

Signature and Confirmation

Signature. You are required to affirm and sign your return or remittance statement by agreeing to the following statement and then providing a voice signature: "I verify and affirm that all tax information provided during this telephone call is correct. I am aware that if any of the information provided by me is knowingly false, I am subject to punishment." Your return or remittance statement cannot be processed without this affirmation or a signature. Tax preparers filing on behalf of clients will also be required to enter their own tax identification number.

Confirmation Number. After you sign your return or remittance statement, stay on the line until the system assigns you a seven-digit confirmation number. This number serves as proof that your filing was completed. Enter the number and the date you filed your return or remittance statement in the boxes on the worksheet for the appropriate period along with the name of the person who "signed" the return or remittance statement. **Your return or remittance statement is not filed until you receive a confirmation number.**

Your confirmation number is your only proof that your return or remittance statement was filed. Enter it on your worksheet and keep the worksheet for your business files for four years in case of audit. **Do not mail it to the Division of Taxation.**

If you file your quarterly return in one phone call, but make your quarterly payment by e-check or EFT debit in a separate call to the Business Paperless Telefiling System, you will receive a separate confirmation number for the payment transaction.

Amended Returns

Errors on monthly remittance statements (Forms ST-51) are to be adjusted on the quarterly return (Form ST-50) for that quarter. Errors on quarterly returns must be corrected by filing an amended return. You may amend a quarterly return through the Business Paperless Telefiling System or online. If the correction results in an overpayment of tax for the quarter, file a Claim for Refund (Form A-3730). To obtain Form A-3730, visit the Division of Taxation website or call the Forms Request System. (See "Where to Get Information" below.)

Where to Get Information
By Phone
Call the Division of Taxation's Customer Service Center at **609-292-6400.**

Online
- Division of Taxation website:
  www.njtaxation.org
- Email general State tax questions:
  nj.taxation@treas.nj.gov
  Do not include confidential information such as Social Security or federal tax identification numbers, liability or payment amounts, dates of birth, or bank account numbers in your email.

Forms and Publications
To obtain copies of the EZ Telefile Worksheet and Instructions, as well as other tax forms and publications:

- Visit the Division of Taxation's website:
  Forms: **www.state.nj.us/treasury/taxation/forms.shtml**
  Publications: **www.state.nj.us/treasury/taxation/pubs.shtml**
- Call the Forms Request System at **800-323-4400** (within NJ, NY, PA, DE, and MD) or **609-826-4400** (touch-tone phones only) to have printed forms or publications mailed to you.

  NOTE: Due to budgetary constraints, supplies are limited and only certain forms and publications can be ordered through this System.

In Person
Visit a New Jersey Division of Taxation regional office. For the address of the office nearest you, call the Automated Tax Information System from a touch-tone phone at **800-323-4400** (within NJ, NY, PA, DE, and MD) or **609-826-4400** or visit our website (www.state.nj.us/treasury/taxation/ot1.shtml).

In the sample form shown on page 45 you would be required to show why you did not collect tax on the $6,071. The State will more than likely audit (when they do) two or three years. This means that eight to twelve quarterly reports will be questioned for accuracy. You must be prepared to show the auditor substantiation for non-taxable sales. Some of the reasons for non-taxable sales might be one or more of the following:

1. **Proof on non-taxable sales (food, clothing, etc.)**

2. **Sales made out of State**

3. **Sales to a tax-exempt organization**

4. **Wholesale sales to retailers**

The State of New is very aggressive in their efforts to collect what is due them. If you cannot provide evidence as to why you did not collect tax, you will be required to pay it. Some of the forms needed to prove non-taxable sales are shown on the following pages.

If you have any questions concerning whether your products or services are taxable or what certificates should be utilized, simply contact the sales tax office nearest you. (See locations listed on page 43.)

At this point, we will review how your records should be kept to provide sufficient information regarding taxable and non-taxable sales.

It is necessary to maintain a record of your receipts or sales by differentiating between taxable and non-taxable sales.

Let's refer back to the Sales Tax form for the months of October, November and December. Here we reported a total sales figure of $18,500 and non-taxable of $6,071. In an audit, the agent reviews your sales tax forms and he/she will ask you to explain why you did not collect sales tax on the $6,071. If you have kept clear records, you simply only have to refer back to the sales or receipts journal to determine where the non-taxable sales were. For each non-taxable sale you need to have an exemption certificate on file or be able to prove an out-of-state sale.

As you can see from the sales journal on this page, the non-taxable sales total $6,071. You would need to keep on file one or more of the following forms: ST-3, ST-4, ST-7, ST-8, or ST-13. These certificates are filled out by the business owner who buys from you and does not pay sales tax. If you can produce these completed certificates, they will usually suffice for the auditor as proof of non-taxable sales.

DATE	INVOICE	TO	AMT	NON TAXABLE	TAXABLE	SALES TAX
10/3	1007	M-M CO	2000	2000		
10/15	1008	CERO-SMIT	1500		1500	103
10/22	1009	M-M CO	500	500		
11/3	1010	ROBYN INC	3100		3100	213
11/17	1011	AMELA CO	700	700		
12/1	1012	JSN CO	800	800		
12/19	1013	METRIC	900		900	62
12/26	1014	LN INC	9000	2071	6929	477
		TOTALS	18500	6071	12429	855

Some of these certificates can be explained as follows:

ST-3   **Resale Certificate – given to a wholesaler by the retailer. The retailer does not pay sales tax because he will resell the item to the final consumer. The final consumer pays the tax.**

ST-4   **Issued by the purchaser who is buying items that are tax exempt.**

ST-7   **Used by farmers for tax-exempt purchases.**

ST-8   **Issued by a homeowner to a contractor. The completed form exempts the homeowner from paying sales tax on capital improvements to the property.**

ST-13   **Issued by a contractor for exempt purchases of material used for real property.**

The forms substantiating non-taxable sales need only be completed once for each purchaser. As an example, one of your customers, the North Edison Little League, purchases hardware supplies from you several times a month. You must keep on file an ST-4 form signed by the Little League. Once you have the form, all subsequent sales are non-taxable by the same organization.

Some of the forms used to prove non-taxable sales are shown on the following pages.

State of New Jersey
DIVISION OF TAXATION

SALES TAX
FORM ST-3

RESALE CERTIFICATE

The seller must collect the tax on a sale of taxable property or services unless the purchaser gives him a properly completed New Jersey exemption certificate.

PURCHASER'S NEW JERSEY
TAXPAYER REGISTRATION NUMBER

To be completed by purchaser and given to and retained by seller. See instructions on back.
Seller should read and comply with the instructions given on both sides of an exemption certificate.

TO _____ Date _____
(Name of Seller)

_____
Address   City   State   Zip

The undersigned certifies that:

(1) He holds a valid Certificate of Authority (number shown above) to collect State of New Jersey Sales and Use Tax.

(2) He is principally engaged in the sale of (indicate nature of merchandise or service sold):

(3) The merchandise or services being herein purchased are described as follows:

(4) The **merchandise** described in (3) above is being purchased: *(check one or more of the blocks which apply)*

   (a) ☐ For resale in its present form.

   (b) ☐ For resale as converted into or as a component part of a product produced by the undersigned.

   (c) ☐ For use in the performance of a taxable service on personal property, where the property which is the subject of this Certificate becomes part of the property being serviced or is later transferred to the purchaser of the service in conjunction with the performance of the service.

(5) The services described in (3) above are being purchased: *(check the block which applies)*

   (a) ☐ By a seller who will either collect the tax or will resell the services.

   (b) ☐ To be performed on personal property held for sale.

I, the undersigned purchaser, have read and complied with the instructions and rules promulgated pursuant to the New Jersey Sales and Use Tax Act with respect to the use of the Resale Certificate, and it is my belief that the seller named herein is not required to collect the sales or use tax on the transaction or transactions covered by this Certificate. The undersigned purchaser hereby swears under the penalties for perjury and false swearing that all of the information shown in this Certificate is true.

NAME OF PURCHASER   (as registered with the New Jersey Division of Taxation)

_____
(Address of Purchaser)

By _____
(Signature of owner, partner, officer of corporation, etc.)   (Title)

MAY BE REPRODUCED
(Front & Back Required)

FORM ST-3 RESALE CERTIFICATE

ST-4 (4-08, R-13)

State of New Jersey
DIVISION OF TAXATION

SALES TAX

ELIGIBLE NONREGISTERED
PURCHASER: SEE INSTRUCTIONS **

PURCHASER'S NEW JERSEY
TAXPAYER REGISTRATION NUMBER

FORM ST-4

EXEMPT USE CERTIFICATE

To be completed by purchaser and given to and retained by seller.
Please read and comply with the instructions given on both sides of this certificate.

Date _____

TO _____
(Name of Seller)

_____
Address   City   State   Zip

The undersigned certifies that there is no requirement to pay the New Jersey Sales and/or Use Tax on the purchase or purchases covered by this Certificate because the tangible personal property or services purchased will be used for an exempt purpose under the Sales & Use Tax Act.

The tangible personal property or services will be used for the following exempt purpose:

The exemption on the sale of the tangible personal property or services to be used for the above described exempt purpose is provided in subsection N.J.S.A. 54:32B- [   ] (See reverse side for listing for principal exempt uses of tangible personal property or services and fill in the block with proper subsection citation).

I, the undersigned purchaser, have read and complied with the instructions and rules promulgated pursuant to the New Jersey Sales and Use Tax Act with respect to the use of the Exempt Use Certificate, and it is my belief that the seller named herein is not required to collect the sales or use tax on the transaction or transactions covered by this Certificate. The undersigned purchaser hereby swears under the penalties for perjury and false swearing that all of the information shown in this Certificate is true.

_____   _____
NAME OF PURCHASER   (as registered with the New Jersey Division of Taxation)

_____
(Address of Purchaser)

By _____

_____   _____
(Signature of owner, partner, officer of corporation, etc.)   (Title)

MAY BE REPRODUCED
(Front & Back Required)

FORM ST-4 EXEMPT USE CERTIFICATE

ST-13 (4-08, R-8)

State of New Jersey
DIVISION OF TAXATION

SALES TAX

CONTRACTOR'S NEW JERSEY
TAX REGISTRATION NUMBER

To be completed by contractor
and retained by seller.

FORM ST-13

CONTRACTOR'S EXEMPT PURCHASE CERTIFICATE

TO: _____

(Name of Seller)   (Date)

_____

(Address of Seller)

The materials, supplies, or services purchased by the undersigned are for exclusive use in erecting structures, or building on, or otherwise improving, altering or repairing real property of the exempt organization, governmental entity, or qualified housing sponsor named below and are exempt from Sales and Use Tax under N.J.S.A. 54:32B-8.22.

THIS CONTRACT COVERS WORK TO BE PERFORMED FOR: (Check one)

☐ EXEMPT ORGANIZATION

Name of Exempt Organization .... _____

Address .... _____

Exempt Organization Number .... _____

☐ NEW JERSEY OR FEDERAL GOVERNMENTAL ENTITY

Name of Governmental Entity .... _____

Address of Governmental Entity .... _____

☐ QUALIFIED HOUSING SPONSOR

Name of Qualified Housing Sponsor .... _____

Address of Qualified Housing Sponsor .. _____

ADDRESS OR LOCATION OF CONTRACT WORK SITE: (property must be owned or leased by one of the above)

_____

I, the undersigned contractor, hereby verify and affirm that all of the information shown on this certificate is true.

_____
Name of Contractor as registered with the New Jersey Division of Taxation

_____
Address of Contractor

_____
Signature of Contractor or Authorized Employee

See INSTRUCTIONS on reverse side

MAY BE REPRODUCED
(Front & Back Required)

FORM ST-13 CONTRACTOR'S EXEMPT PURCHASE CERTIFICATE

ST-8 (1-08, R-12)

State of New Jersey
DIVISION OF TAXATION

SALES TAX
FORM ST-8

To be completed by both owner of real property and contractor, and retained by contractor. Read instructions on back of this certificate. Do not send this form to the Division of Taxation.

A registered New Jersey contractor must collect the tax on the amount charged for labor and services under the contract unless the owner gives him a properly completed Certificate of Exempt Capital Improvement.

CERTIFICATE OF EXEMPT
CAPITAL IMPROVEMENT

MAY BE ISSUED ONLY BY THE OWNER OF THE REAL PROPERTY
MAY NOT BE ISSUED FOR THE PURCHASE OF MATERIALS

_____
(Name of Contractor)

_____
(Address of Contractor)

_____
(Contractor's New Jersey Certificate of Authority Number)

THE FOLLOWING INFORMATION MUST BE FURNISHED:

The nature of the contract is as follows (describe the exempt capital improvement to be made):_____

_____

_____

_____

_____

The address or location where work is to be performed: _____

_____

TOTAL AMOUNT OF CONTRACT $ _____

The undersigned hereby certifies that he is not required to pay sales and use tax with respect to charges for installation of tangible personal property, because the performance of the contract will result in an exempt capital improvement to real property. The undersigned purchaser hereby affirms (under the penalties for perjury and false swearing) that all of the information shown in this Certificate is true.

CONTRACTOR'S CERTIFICATION	**PROPERTY OWNER'S SIGNATURE**
I certify that all sales and use tax due has been or will be paid by the undersigned on purchases of materials incorporated or consumed in the performance of the contract described herein.	_____ (Name of owner of real property) _____ (Address of owner of real property) By _____
_____ _____ (Signature of Contractor) (Date)	_____ _____ (Signature of owner, partner, (Date) officer of corporation, etc.)

Any person making representations on this certificate which are willfully false may be subject to such penalties as may be provided for by law.

REPRODUCTION OF CERTIFICATE OF EXEMPT CAPITAL IMPROVEMENT FORMS: Private reproduction of both sides of the Exempt Capital Improvement Certificates may be made without the prior permission of the Division of Taxation.

FORM ST-8 CERTIFICATE OF CAPITAL IMPROVEMENT

ST-7 (1-08, R-11)

| Purchaser's New Jersey Tax Registration Number | **State of New Jersey**
DIVISION OF TAXATION

SALES TAX | Eligible Nonregistered Purchaser
(See Instructions) |

FORM ST-7

FARMER'S EXEMPTION CERTIFICATE

To be completed by purchaser and given to and retained by seller.

The seller must collect the tax on a sale of taxable property or services unless the purchaser gives him a properly completed New Jersey exemption certificate.

TO _____ Date _____

(Name of Seller)

_____

(Address)

_____

(City)   (State)   (Zip)

Check applicable box:

☐ Single Purchase Certificate

☐ Blanket Certificate

The purchaser certifies that it is exempt from payment of the Sales and Use Tax on purchases to be made from the seller because the property or service is to be used for an exempt purpose described in N.J.S.A. 54:32B-8.16 of the Sales and Use Tax Act as follows:

"Sales of tangible personal property and production and conservation services to a farmer for use and consumption directly and primarily in the production, handling and preservation for sale of agricultural or horticultural commodities at the farming enterprise of that farmer."

Description of agricultural or horticultural commodities produced at the purchaser's farmer enterprise:

_____

_____

Description of tangible personal property or service purchased: _____

_____

_____

(Name of individual, partnership, association, or corporation)

_____

(Business address)

By _____

(Signature of individual farm owner, partner, officer of corporation or other qualified representative)

INSTRUCTIONS

This certificate must be presented to a seller when making an exempt purchase. The farmer's exemption does not apply to purchases which will not be used directly and primarily in farm production. The purchases of automobiles, certain other motor vehicles, natural gas, electricity and any materials used to build a building or structure (except silos, greenhouses, grain bins and manure handling facilities) are taxable regardless of the intended use on a farm or by a farmer.

MAY BE REPRODUCED
(Front & Back Required)

FORM ST-7 FARMER'S EXEMPTION CERTIFICATE

8
PAYROLL REPORTING
TO THE
INTERNAL REVENUE SERVICE
AND THE STATE OF NEW JERSEY

In this section on payroll reporting, I will explain some of the payroll reports that must be filed with the I.R.S. and the State of New Jersey. It is important that you be aware of what taxes you are liable for, when they are due, and at what point in time you must inform the federal and state agencies that you have employees.

Payroll Reporting to the Internal Revenue Service

As soon as you have your first employee (full - or part-time), you will need to determine how much tax should be withheld from his/her gross pay. The I.R.S. supplies employers with a booklet called *Circular E*, and it can be obtained from any I.R.S. office. This small pamphlet shows you how much federal withholding tax and social security should be withheld from each employee's pay check. The I.R.S. has requirements for sending them the Federal Withholding Tax and Social Security withheld from your employees.

At least every three months (at the end of a three-month quarter) you may be required to prepare and submit a 941 form. On this form you show how much tax was withheld from the employee's gross pay and remit the amount to the I.R.S. If the taxes withheld from employees exceed $500 in any quarter, you must pay these taxes monthly by using a Federal Tax Deposit Card. This form is shown on the next page. When you file the 941 form, you can take credit for any monthly payment made. Once again, these forms are tough to learn on your own, so let an accountant show you how to complete them the first time.

For any Federal Business Tax information contact the local I.R.S. office at (631) 447-4955 or Fax at (631) 447-8960.

WHEN TO MAKE <u>FORM 940</u> DEPOSITS?

> If the tax liability is $500 or less and it is the end of the first, second, or third quarter, the tax is carried over to the next quarter.

> If the fourth quarter tax liability is $500 or less, the tax is due by the return due date and can be deposited or paid with the return.

> If the tax liability is over $500 and it is the end of any quarter, then the tax must be deposited by the last day of the following month.

HOW TO MAKE DEPOSITS

1. Federal Tax Deposits (FTDs) are made through the Electronic Federal Tax Payment System (EFTPS). EFTPS is a free service provided by the Department of Treasury. It is a convenient and efficient method of paying all your federal taxes. You may make your tax deposit payments through the Internet at www.eftps.gov or call EFTPS Voice Response System at 1-800-555-3453. For added convenience EFTPS is available 24 hours a day, seven days a week.

   New employers receiving a new Employer Identification Number (EIN) that have a federal tax obligation are automatically enrolled in EFTPS to make their Federal Tax Deposits.

   When new employers receive their EIN, they will also receive a separate mailing containing an EFTPS Personal Identification Number (PIN) and instructions for activating their enrollment.

2. As of January 1, 2011, all deposits are made electronically.

WHERE TO MAKE DEPOSITS

Federal Tax Deposits can be made electronically through EFTPS by phone 1-800-555-3453 or visit www.eftps.gov. You should initiate your payment no later than 8:00 p.m. Eastern Time the business day before your deposit is due.

FOR MORE INFORMATION ON FTDs, REFER TO:

EFTPS Customer Service 1-800-555-4477

EFTPS at www.eftps.gov

www.irs.gov

Publication 15, Circular E, Employer's Tax Guide

Publication 966, Electronic Choices for Paying All Your Federal Taxes

Your tax professional

ELECTRONIC FEDERAL TAX PAYMENT SYSTEM (EFTPS)

Q What is EFTPS?

A EFTPS is a tax payment system provided free by the U.S. Department of the Treasury. EFTPS makes paying federal taxes easy and convenient. By using EFTPS, taxpayers make their federal tax payments electronically from the convenience of office or home via the Internet or phone.

Q Who can use EFTPS?

A Anyone who pays federal taxes may voluntarily enroll in and use EFTPS. Taxpayers who are required to deposit taxes must make all their federal tax deposits electronically.

Q How do you enroll?

A New employers are automatically enrolled in EFTPS Express Enrollment. If you would you like to enroll call EFTPS Customer Service at 1-800-555-4477 or visit www.eftps.gov.

Q What is Express Enrollment?

A Express Enrollment allows new business taxpayers with a federal tax obligation to begin making their FTDs more quickly and accurately with EFTPS. When they receive an Employer Identification Number (EIN) from the IRS, they will be enrolled in EFTPS so they can make all their payments electronically, online or by phone.

Q Can businesses still use FTD Coupons?

A Starting January 1, 2011, taxpayers cannot use FTD coupons.

Publication 3151 (Rev. 1-2011) Catalog Number 26404W
Department of Treasury **Internal Revenue Service** www.irs.gov

Form **941 for 2017:** Employer's QUARTERLY Federal Tax Return   950117

(Rev. January 2017)   Department of the Treasury — Internal Revenue Service   OMB No. 1545-0029

Employer identification number (EIN) ☐☐ - ☐☐☐☐☐☐☐

Name (not your trade name)

Trade name (if any)

Address
Number   Street   Suite or room number

City   State   ZIP code

Foreign country name   Foreign province/county   Foreign postal code

Report for this Quarter of 2017
(Check one.)

☐ 1: January, February, March

☐ 2: April, May, June

☐ 3: July, August, September

☐ 4: October, November, December

Instructions and prior year forms are available at www.irs.gov/form941.

Read the separate instructions before you complete Form 941. Type or print within the boxes.

Part 1:   Answer these questions for this quarter.

1   Number of employees who received wages, tips, or other compensation for the pay period including: *Mar. 12* (Quarter 1), *June 12* (Quarter 2), *Sept. 12* (Quarter 3), or *Dec. 12* (Quarter 4)   **1** [   ]

2   Wages, tips, and other compensation . . . .   **2** [   ]

3   Federal income tax withheld from wages, tips, and other compensation . . . . . .   **3** [   ]

4   If no wages, tips, and other compensation are subject to social security or Medicare tax   ☐ Check and go to line 6.

		Column 1		Column 2
5a	Taxable social security wages . .	[ ]	× 0.124 =	[ ]
5b	Taxable social security tips . . .	[ ]	× 0.124 =	[ ]
5c	Taxable Medicare wages & tips. .	[ ]	× 0.029 =	[ ]
5d	Taxable wages & tips subject to Additional Medicare Tax withholding	[ ]	× 0.009 =	[ ]

5e   Add Column 2 from lines 5a, 5b, 5c, and 5d . . . .   **5e** [   ]

5f   Section 3121(q) Notice and Demand—Tax due on unreported tips (see instructions) . .   **5f** [   ]

6   Total taxes before adjustments. Add lines 3, 5e, and 5f . . . .   **6** [   ]

7   Current quarter's adjustment for fractions of cents . . . .   **7** [   ]

8   Current quarter's adjustment for sick pay . . . .   **8** [   ]

9   Current quarter's adjustments for tips and group-term life insurance . . . . . .   **9** [   ]

10   Total taxes after adjustments. Combine lines 6 through 9 . . . .   **10** [   ]

11   Qualified small business payroll tax credit for increasing research activities. Attach Form 8974   **11** [   ]

12   Total taxes after adjustments and credits. Subtract line 11 from line 10 . . . . . .   **12** [   ]

13   Total deposits for this quarter, including overpayment applied from a prior quarter and overpayments applied from Form 941-X, 941-X (PR), 944-X, or 944-X (SP) filed in the current quarter   **13** [   ]

14   Balance due. If line 12 is more than line 13, enter the difference and see instructions . . .   **14** [   ]

15   Overpayment. If line 13 is more than line 12, enter the difference [   ] Check one: ☐ Apply to next return.   ☐ Send a refund.

▶ **You MUST complete both pages of Form 941 and SIGN it.**   Next ▶

For Privacy Act and Paperwork Reduction Act Notice, see the back of the Payment Voucher.   Cat. No. 17001Z   Form **941** (Rev. 1-2017)

Name (not your trade name)   Employer identification number (EIN)   950217

If you are unsure about whether you are a monthly schedule depositor or a semiweekly schedule depositor, see section 11 of Pub. 15.

16 Check one: ☐ Line 12 on this return is less than $2,500 or line 12 (line 10 if the prior quarter was the fourth quarter of 2016) on the return for the prior quarter was less than $2,500, and you didn't incur a $100,000 next-day deposit obligation during the current quarter. If line 12 (line 10 if the prior quarter was the fourth quarter of 2016) for the prior quarter was less than $2,500 but line 12 on this return is $100,000 or more, you must provide a record of your federal tax liability. If you are a monthly schedule depositor, complete the deposit schedule below; if you are a semiweekly schedule depositor, attach Schedule B (Form 941). Go to Part 3.

☐ You were a monthly schedule depositor for the entire quarter. Enter your tax liability for each month and total liability for the quarter, then go to Part 3.

Tax liability: Month 1 [   ] .

              Month 2 [   ] .

              Month 3 [   ] .

Total liability for quarter [   ] .   Total must equal line 12.

☐ You were a semiweekly schedule depositor for any part of this quarter. Complete Schedule B (Form 941), Report of Tax Liability for Semiweekly Schedule Depositors, and attach it to Form 941.

17 If your business has closed or you stopped paying wages . . . . ☐ Check here, and

enter the final date you paid wages [/   /   ] .

18 If you are a seasonal employer and you don't have to file a return for every quarter of the year . . ☐ Check here.

Do you want to allow an employee, a paid tax preparer, or another person to discuss this return with the IRS? See the instructions for details.

☐ Yes. Designee's name and phone number [   ]   [   ]

Select a 5-digit Personal Identification Number (PIN) to use when talking to the IRS. ☐ ☐ ☐ ☐ ☐

☐ No.

Under penalties of perjury, I declare that I have examined this return, including accompanying schedules and statements, and to the best of my knowledge and belief, it is true, correct, and complete. Declaration of preparer (other than taxpayer) is based on all information of which preparer has any knowledge.

X Sign your name here [   ]

Print your name here [   ]

Print your title here [   ]

Date [/   /   ]

Best daytime phone [   ]

Paid Preparer Use Only   Check if you are self-employed . . . ☐

Preparer's name [   ]

PTIN [   ]

Preparer's signature [   ]

Date [/   /   ]

Firm's name (or yours if self-employed) [   ]

EIN [   ]

Address [   ]

Phone [   ]

City [   ] State [   ]

ZIP code [   ]

Form **941** (Rev. 1-2017)

Payroll Reporting to the State of New Jersey

Like any other state agency, New Jersey has a form to be completed for payroll-reporting procedures. In New Jersey you are required to notify the state as soon as your gross payroll reaches $1,000. This will also alert the Division of Unemployment and Disability so that your employee will be eligible for benefits. If you did not complete a NJ-REG form when you started your business, you do that and answer question one with the appropriate informaiton. If you had already completed a form NJ-REG, you file an amended application and answer the questions on page two.

From your employees you are obligated to withhold the New Jersey Gross Income Tax and a combination of Unemployment/Disability. You may contact the New Jersey Department of Labor and Industry, CN 390, Trenton, New Jersey 08625 to obtain the N.J.G.I.T. withholding tax tables. At the time this book was written, New Jersey also required the employee to pay .0825% of his/her gross pay toward unemployment/disability to the state for wages paid up to $33,500. The employer withholds this from the employee's gross pay, and matches it according to a formula based on claims made by former employees for unemployment and/or disability benefits.

New Jersey requires a quarterly reporting just as the I.R.S. and there are two forms that must be completed and mailed at the end of a three-month quarter. They are the NJ-927 and NJ500. The NJ-500 reports monthly withholding tax and the NJ-927 reports quarterly wages, withholding tax, and is used to remit payments for unemployment and disability amounts.

If your New Jersey Gross income tax withheld from employees exceeds $500 per month, you must file monthly. The filing and payment will need to be completed online electronically. The website is: www.state.nj.us/treasury/revenue/electronicfileopt.shtml/

Remember, as soon as you have employees, it will be necessary to begin filing the necessary forms with the I.R.S. and the State of New Jersey. Don't delay doing this, as you are subject to penalties for non-filing and interest for all withholding taxes not paid timely.

Just a reminder. In all states you are obligated to carry worker's compensation insurance as soon as you hire your first employee.

You may obtain information regarding worker's compensation by calling (609) 292-2516 or (973) 622-6014 or by writing to the

Division of Worker's Compensation
Department of Labor
CN381
Trenton, New Jersey 08625

NJ-REG	STATE OF NEW JERSEY	MAIL TO:
3-2011	DIVISION OF REVENUE	CLIENT REGISTRATION PO BOX 252 TRENTON, NJ 08646-0252

NJ-REG
3-2011

STATE OF NEW JERSEY
DIVISION OF REVENUE
BUSINESS REGISTRATION APPLICATION
Please read instructions carefully before filling out this form
ALL SECTIONS MUST BE FULLY COMPLETED

' NO FEE REQUIRED '

MAIL TO:
CLIENT REGISTRATION
PO BOX 252
TRENTON, NJ 08646-0252

OVERNIGHT DELIVERY:
CLIENT REGISTRATION
33 West State St 3rd FL
TRENTON, NJ 08608

Hotline
(609) 292-9292
www.nj.gov/treasury/revenue/

REGISTRATION DETAIL

A. Please indicate the reason for your filing this application:
- ☐ Original application for a new business
- ☐ Moved previously registered business to new location (REG-C-L can be used in lieu of NJ-REG)
- ☒ Amended application for an existing business *STARTING PAYROLL*
  Reason(s) for amending application:
- ☐ Application for an additional location of an existing registered business
- ☐ Applying for a Business Registration Certificate ☐ Employer of Domestic Household Employee(s)
- ☐ Withholding for Employee(s) residing in NJ (Not doing business or employing in NJ)

B. FEIN # `2` `2` `2` `2` `2` `2` `2` `2` OR Soc. Sec. # of Owner ☐☐☐ ☐☐ ☐☐☐☐
☐ Check Box if "Applied for"

C. Name *JON AND AMY CARLIN*
(If your business entity is a Corporation, LLC, LLP, LP or Non-Profit Organization, give entity name. IF NOT, give Name of Owner or Partners)

D. Trade Name *JAMY'S DONUT SHOPPE*

E. Business Location: (Do not use P.O. Box for Location Address)
Street *44 DONNA COURT*
City *CLARK* State `N` `J`
Zip Code `0` `7` `0` `6` `6` `1` `2` `3` `4`
(Give 9-digit Zip)
(See instructions for providing alternate addresses)

F. Mailing Name and Address: (if different from business address)
Name
Street
City _____ State ☐☐
Zip Code ☐☐☐☐☐ ☐☐☐☐
(Give 9-digit Zip)

BUSINESS DETAIL

G. Beginning date for this business: `1` / `1` / `17` (see instructions)
month / day / year
O/C ___

H. Type of ownership (check one):
- ☐ NJ Corporation ☐ Sole Proprietor ☒ Partnership ☐ Out-of-State Corporation ☐ LLP ☐ Other
- ☐ Limited Partnership ☐ LLC (1065 Filer) ☐ LLC (1120 Filer) ☐ LLC (Single Member) ☐ S Corporation (You must complete page 41)

I. New Jersey Business Code `5` `3` `0` `6` (see instructions) ☐ Domestic Household Employer

J. County / Municipality Code `2` `0` `0` `2` (see instructions) K. County *UNION*
(New Jersey only)

FOR OFFICIAL USE ONLY
DLN ___

L. Will this business be SEASONAL? ☐ Yes ☒ No
If YES - Circle months business will be open:
JAN FEB MAR   APR MAY JUN   JUL AUG SEPT   OCT NOV DEC

M. If an ENTITY (item C) complete the following:
Date of Incorporation: ___ / ___ / ___   State of Incorporation ☐☐   Fiscal month ☐☐
month / day / year
NJ Business/Corp. # ☐☐☐☐ ☐☐☐☐ ☐☐☐

Is this a Subsidiary of another corporation? ☐ YES ☐ NO
If YES, give name and Federal ID# of parent: ___

N. Standard Industrial Code ☐☐☐☐ (If known)   O. NAICS ☐☐☐☐☐ (If known)

P. Provide the following information for the owner, partners or responsible corporate officers. (If more space is needed, attach rider)

OWNERSHIP DETAIL

NAME (Last Name, First, MI)	SOCIAL SECURITY NUMBER TITLE	HOME ADDRESS (Street, City, State, Zip)	PERCENT OF OWNERSHIP
CARLIN, JON	*111-11-1111* *PARTNER*	*76 EAST WAY* *LINCROFT, NJ 07738*	*50*
CARLIN, AMY	*222-22-2222* *PARTNER*	*76 EAST WAY* *LINCROFT, NJ 07738*	*50*

BE SURE TO COMPLETE NEXT PAGE

- 17 -

N.J. REG - AMENDED RETURN
TO REPORT NEW PAYROLL

FEIN#: 22-2222222   NAME: JON AND AMY CARLIN   NJ-REG

Each Question Must Be Answered Completely

1. a. Have you or will you be paying wages, salaries or commissions to employees working in New Jersey within the next 6 months? .... ☒ Yes ☐ No

   Give date of first wage or salary payment: 1 , 8 , 17
                                 Month   Day   Year

   If you answered "No" to question 1.a., please be aware that if you begin paying wages you are required to notify the Client Registration Bureau at PO Box 252, Trenton NJ 08646-0252, or phone (609)-292-9292.

   b. Give date of hiring first NJ employee: ____ / ____ / ____
                                Month   Day   Year

   c. Date cumulative gross payroll exceeds $1,000   1 , 15 , 17
                                   Month   Day   Year

   d. Will you be paying wages, salaries or commissions to New Jersey residents working outside New Jersey? .... ☐ Yes ☒ No

   e. Will you be the payer of pension or annuity income to New Jersey residents? .... ☐ Yes ☒ No

   f. Will you be holding legalized games of chance in New Jersey (as defined in Chapter 47 Rules of Legalized Games of Chance) where proceeds from any one prize exceed $1,000? .... ☐ Yes ☒ No

   g. Is this business a PEO (Employee Leasing Company)?   (If yes, see page 6) .... ☐ Yes ☒ No

2. Did you acquire ☐ Substantially all the assets; ☐ Trade or business; ☐ Employees; of any previous employing units? .... ☐ Yes ☒ No
   If answer is "No", go to question 4.
   If answer is "Yes", indicate by a check whether ☐ in whole or ☐ in part, and list business name, address and registration number of predecessor or acquired unit and the date business was acquired by you. (If more than one, list separately. Continue on separate sheet if necessary.)

   Name of Acquired Unit _____

                                          N.J. Employer ID   ACQUIRED   PERCENTAGE ACQUIRED
                                                      ☐ Assets _____ %

   Address _____   Date Acquired _____   ☐ Trade or Business _____ %
                                                      ☐ Employees _____ %

3. Subject to certain regulations, the law provides for the transfer of the predecessor's employment experience to a successor where the whole of a business is acquired from a subject predecessor employer. The transfer of the employment experience is required by law.

   Are the predecessor and successor units owned or controlled by the same interests? .... ☐ Yes ☒ No

4. Is your employment agricultural? .... ☐ Yes ☒ No

5. Is your employment household? .... ☐ Yes ☒ No

   a. If yes, please indicate the date in the calendar quarter in which gross cash wages totaled $1,000 or more ____ / ____ / ____
                                                          Month   Day   Year

6. Are you a 501(c)(3) organization? .... ☐ Yes ☒ No
   If "Yes", to apply for sales tax exemption, obtain form REG-1E at http://www.state.nj.us/treasury/taxation/pdf/other_forms/sales/reg1e.pdf

7. Were you subject to the Federal Unemployment Tax Act (FUTA) in the current or preceding calendar year? .... ☐ Yes ☒ No

   (See instruction sheet for explanation of FUTA) If "Yes", indicate year: _____

8. a. Does this employing unit claim exemption from liability for contributions under the Unemployment Compensation Law of New Jersey? .... ☐ Yes ☒ No

   If "Yes," please state reason. (Use additional sheets if necessary.) _____

   b. If exemption from the mandatory provisions of the Unemployment Compensation Law of New Jersey is claimed, does this employing unit wish to voluntarily elect to become subject to its provisions for a period of not less than two complete calendar years? .... ☐ Yes ☐ No

9. Type of business   ☐ 1. Manufacturer   ☐ 2. Service   ☐ 3. Wholesale
                     ☐ 4. Construction   ☒ 5. Retail   ☐ 6. Government

   Principal product or service in New Jersey only __BAKED GOODS_____
   Type of Activity in New Jersey only __BAKERY_____

10. List below each place of business and each class of industry in New Jersey, even though you may have only one place of business or engage in only one class of industry.

   a. Do you have more than one employing facility in New Jersey? .... ☐ Yes ☐ No

NJ WORK LOCATIONS (Physical location, not mailing address)		NATURE OF BUSINESS (See Instructions)			No. of Workers at Each Location and/in Each Class of Industry
Street Address, City, Zip Code	County	NAICS Code	Principal Product or Service Complete Description	%	
44 DONNA COURT CLARK, NJ 07066	UNION	5306	BAKERY	100	1

(Continue on separate sheet, if necessary)

BE SURE TO COMPLETE NEXT PAGE
- 18 -

N.J. REG - AMENDED RETURN TO REPORT NEW PAYROLL
(CONTINUED)

New Jersey New Hire Reporting Form

Federal and state legislation (N.J.S.A. 2A: 17-56.61) requires all New Jersey employers, both public and private, to report to the State of New Jersey all newly hired, contracted, rehired, or returning to work employees. Information about new hire reporting and online reporting is available on our website: **www.nj-newhire.com**

Send completed forms to:
New Jersey New Hire Directory
PO Box 4654 Trenton, NJ 08650-4901
Toll-free fax: 800-304-4901

To ensure the highest level of accuracy, please print neatly in capital letters and avoid contact with the edges of the boxes. The following will serve as an example:

| A | B | C | | 1 | 2 | 3 |

EMPLOYER INFORMATION

Federal Employer ID Number (FEIN): *(Please enter the same FEIN used to report the employee's quarterly wages)*

Employer Name:

Employer Address:

Employer City: State: Zip Code:

Employer Phone (optional):   Extension: Employer Fax (optional):

Email Address:

EMPLOYEE INFORMATION

Employee Social Security Number (SSN):

Is this employee an Independent Contractor?
Yes   No

Employee First Name: Middle Initial

Employee Last Name:

Employee Address:

Employee City: State: Zip Code:

Date of Hire (MMDDYY):*   Date of Birth (MMDDYY):   *Date of Hire is defined as the date an employee first performed services for pay.

Reports must be submitted within 20 days of hire or rehire date. Failure to report could result in a fine.

REPORTS WILL NOT BE PROCESSED IF REQUIRED INFORMATION IS MISSING

Questions? Call us at (609) 631-0330 or toll-free at (877) NJ-HIRES

Rev 3/12

N.J. NEW HIRE FORM

Forms, Fees, & Instructions

Division of Revenue   NJBGS

Instructions for Completing Employer Payroll Tax Form NJ-927

General Instructions

The NJ-927 Form has been revised for reporting periods starting with the
report for the 3rd quarter of 1998 (report due October 30, 1998). The
revised form will be scanned and imaged using automated character
recognition technologies to input the information you supply. Please read
and follow all instructions carefully.

The New Jersey Taxpayers' Bill Of Rights

The Taxpayers' Bill of Rights became law as P.L. 1992,c.175. The intent of
the legislation is to insure that all taxpayers receive the information and
assistance they need to understand and meet their State tax
responsibilities and to insure that they receive fair and equal treatment in
their dealings with the New Jersey Division of Taxation. By extension, the
Division of Revenue is committed to complying with this legislation.

Information on the Taxpayers' Bill of Rights is available through the
Division of Taxation. Call 1-800-323-4400 (Touch-tone phones within New
Jersey only) or (609) 588-2525 (Touch-tone phones anywhere) to order
Taxation's publication, ANJ-1, New Jersey Taxpayers' Bill of Rights
(ANJ-1).

Customer service representatives are available at both the Division of
Taxation and the Department of Labor to answer specific tax questions
about the Gross Income Tax (Taxation) and Unemployment and Disability
Insurance (Division of Employer Accounts). Those general information
phone numbers are:

Division of Employer Accounts Hotline (609) 633-6400
Division of Taxation Hotline (609) 292-6400

You can find information, and answers to frequently asked questions on
the following Web sites:

NJ Division of Taxation - http://www.state.nj.us/treasury/taxation
NJ Department of Labor - http://www.state.nj.us/labor

INSTRUCTIONS FOR COMPLETING
THE N.J. TAX FORM 927

STATE OF NEW JERSEY
EMPLOYER REPORT OF WAGES PAID
Read instructions on reverse side of employer's copy before completing this report.

WR-30 (R-7-04)

New Jersey Employer Registration Number:			Quarter Ending		Report Due		Tape Auth. No.	

Federal Employer I.D. Number:

Municipal Code:

Industry Code:

Total No. of Employees Reported			Total Gross Wages Reported	$	

	(1) Employee Social Security Number	(2) Employee Name (Last, First, MI)	(3) Gross Wages Paid	(4) Base Weeks During Which Employee Earned $ or more
1				
2				
3				
4				
5				
6				
7				
8				
9				
10				
11				
12				
13				
14				
15				
16				

I certify the information in this report is true and correct.

X _____

(Signature)   (Title)   (Date)   (____) _____ (Telephone)

Do Not Use This Form To Make Additions or Corrections
MAY BE REPRODUCED

Page _____ of _____ Pages

THE N.J. STATUS REPORT OF WAGES PAID

71

INSTRUCTIONS FOR FILING THE EMPLOYER REPORT OF WAGES PAID (WR-30)

1. GENERAL INSTRUCTIONS

The Division of Revenue will issue pre-printed wage reporting forms (Form WR-30) to all New Jersey employers who reported 100 or fewer employees in the previous quarter. Since pre-printed forms contain the name and Social Security Number of each employee, employers need to record only gross wages paid and base weeks earned within the data boxes on the form. The employee information on the pre-printed Form WR-30 should not be substituted by attaching a separate printout. For new employees, each pre-printed WR-30 will have an ADD Form on the back of the page. The ADD Form must be used to add new employees who are being reported for the first time. Employees must be added, even if you reported them under the federal New Hire Program. The New Hire Program became effective March 5, 1998 and is federally mandated. If you have questions about the New Hire Program, please call (toll free) 877-NJ- HIRES. Please do not use the front of the form to add employees.

Total Gross Wages Reported This Quarter: Enter the total gross wages paid to all employees included in the report for this quarter.

Total New Employees ADDED: Enter the total number of new employees you included on the ADD Form.

Total Employees Reported This Quarter: Add the number of new employees to the number of employees pre-printed on the WR-30. Enter the total number of employees (minus those deleted) to be reported for this quarter.

A. Social Security Number

The Social Security Number for each of your employees should be pre-printed in Column A on the form, if it was reported for the previous quarter. The Social Security Number should read exactly as it appears on the employee's Social Security Card. If the employee's Social Security Number is incorrect, fill in the oval in Column C, and enter all the employee's correct information on the ADD page.

B. Employee Name

The employee name should be pre-printed in the following sequence: Last Name, First Name, Middle Initial in Column B of the employee portion of the report. The employee name and Social Security Number should appear only once on any quarterly return. To correct an employee's name, fill in the oval in Column C, and enter all the employee's correct information on the ADD page.

C. Delete Column

On the re-designed Form WR-30, the delete column is now Column C (an oval shaped box) located between the Employee Name and Quarterly Gross Wages Paid columns. If an employee listed should not be reported, fill in the oval in Column C.

D. Quarterly Gross Wages Paid

Enter the employee gross wages within the data boxes in Column D, "Quarterly Gross Wages Paid." Please do not use commas, decimal points or any other symbols in or between the boxes. If no wages were paid, enter zero (0). Leaving this column blank will generate a penalty.

E. Base Weeks

Enter in Column E the number of base weeks during which the employee earned remuneration in an amount equal to or more than the amount shown above Column E on the front of the form. Base weeks listed for an employee can not exceed the maximum allowable base weeks shown in the message box on Form WR-30. If an employee did not earn any base weeks for the quarter being reported, you must enter a zero (0). Leaving this column blank will generate a penalty.

9
INCORPORATING YOUR BUSINESS IN NEW JERSEY

I like to tell a story of the business owner who comes to me to set up the books for a new corporation. My first question is always: Why did you incorporate? The answer varies and goes something like this – "Well, I thought it was a good idea" or "My friends told me I needed a corporation" or "I read somewhere that it would save me taxes."

There are many reasons to incorporate and just as many not to do it. Before you make the decision to incorporate, make sure you know why you are making the decision.

When you incorporate, you get permission from the State to create a separate business entity that can operate a business in N.J. This new entity has the right to enter into contracts, sue or be sued, and own property. Ownership of the corporation is shown by shares of stock issued to the stockholders.

The major advantages are as follows:
1. **You can limit your liability**
   If you incorporate, under most situations, your personal assets are safe from obligations incurred by the corporation. But the corporate form will not limit your liability for wrongdoings or on loans which you may have personally guaranteed.

2. **Lower tax rates**
   Depending on your personal income, the corporation may be advantageous to keep your taxes to a minimum.

3. **Raise capital through sale of stocks and bonds**
   The corporate structure allows the owners to raise money by selling stocks and borrow money through bond sales.

4. **Sometimes easier to borrow money**
   As a corporation, the lending institutions may charge a higher rate of interest than that allowed to an individual. The bank, therefore, may be willing to lend your corporation money because they can collect more interest.

5. **Welfare plans**
   In many situations, the corporation will be able to deduct expenditures that would not be allowed as a sole proprietor or partnership. Examples are: medical bills, disability insurance, and group life insurance when included in qualified welfare programs for employees.

6. **Easy to transfer ownership**
   You can sell ownership in the corporation by transferring your shares of stock.

7. **Continued existence**
   Once formed, the corporation continues regardless of who may own the stock. But in reality, the corporation may actually be worthless if the major controlling stockholder is unable to work in the business.

8. **High pension plan deductions**
   Presently, the corporate structure may allow greater pension plan expenses than a sole proprietor or partnership.

9. **Looks classy to your customers**
   The corporate structure and name shown with Inc. or Corp. following the title infers a large company. This type of title may impress people more than a sole proprietor.

The disadvantages are:
1. **Initial costs are high**
   The expenses to incorporate a business are significantly higher than starting a sole proprietor or partnership. Costs range from $100 to $1,000 depending on your business and the amount of work completed by your attorney.

2. **Professional fees are costly**
   The accounting and legal fees to maintain a corporation are much more expensive than those of a sole proprietor or partnership.

3. **High taxes**
   In many instances, you will have to pay corporate taxes to the I.R.S. and the State of New Jersey.

4. **Higher payroll taxes**
   The stockholders receiving compensation from the corporation will be considered employees and must pay Federal Social

Security and New Jersey Unemployment. The corporate structure will result in higher payroll taxes than the sole proprietor or partnership organization.

5. **May be personally liable**
   Even though the business is incorporated and has limited liability, you may still be required to sign personally for loans and contracts.

If you decide to incorporate or form an LLC in the State of New Jersey, you need to file and complete the Public Records Filing form. The form can be obtained from the State web site at https://www.nj.gov/treasury/revenue/gettingregistered.htm. You may also use the site to complete the application and form your new business entity on line.

You may also fax a completed form to the State Treasurer at 609-984-6851. Be sure to include a cover letter with your requested business name, a return fax number, and your personal credit card information.

Obtaining a Name for Your Corporation or Limited Liability Company
By calling the New Jersey State Treasurer, Division of Commercial Recording, you can do a search of potential names for your Corporation or Limited Partnership within minutes. The Division has recently installed a new telephone system with several options. The phone number is 1-866-534-7789.

You may also check the availability of a name by visiting the NJ web site at: http://www.state.nj.us/treasury/revenue/checkbusiness.htm.

You can also download the application from the NJ Website Business Portal at : www.newjerseybusiness.gov.

STATE OF NEW JERSEY
DIVISION OF REVENUE

"FEE REQUIRED"   **PUBLIC RECORDS FILING FOR NEW BUSINESS ENTITY**

Fill out all information below INCLUDING INFORMATION FOR ITEM 11, and sign in the space provided. Please note that once filed, this form constitutes your original certificate of incorporation/formation/registration/authority, and the information contained in the filed form is considered public. Refer to the instructions for delivery/return options, filing fees and field-by-field requirements. Remember to remit the appropriate fee amount. Use attachments if more space is required for any field, or if you wish to add articles for the public record.

1. **Business Name:** JON and AMY CARLIN

2. **Type of Business Entity:** ___ ___ ___
   (See Instructions for Codes, Page 21, Item 2)

3. **Business Purpose :**
   (See Instructions, Page 22, Item 3)

4. **Stock** (Domestic Corporations only; LLCs and Non-Profit leave blank):

5. **Duration** (If Indefinite or Perpetual, leave bank):

6. **State of Formation/Incorporation** (Foreign Entities Only):

7. **Date of Formation/Incorporation** (Foreign Entities Only):

8. **Contact Information:**
   Registered Agent Name: _____

   Registered Office:
   (Must be a New Jersey street address)

   Main Business or Principal Business Address:

   Street _____

   Street _____

   City _____ Zip _____

   City _____ State _____ Zip _____

9. **Management** (Domestic Corporations and Limited Partnerships Only)
   - For-Profit and Professional Corporations list initial Board of Directors, minimum of 1;
   - Domestic Non-Profits list Board of Trustees, minimum of 3;
   - Limited Partnerships list all General Partners.

Name	Street Address	City	State	Zip

The signatures below certify that the business entity has complied with all applicable filing requirements pursuant to the laws of the State of New Jersey.

10. **Incorporators** (Domestic Corporations Only, minimum of 1)

Name	Street Address	City	State	Zip

Signature(s) for the Public Record (See instructions for Information on Signature Requirements)

Signature	Name	Title	Date

CERTIFICATE OF INCORPORATION

INSTRUCTIONS FOR BUSINESS ENTITY PUBLIC RECORD FILING

GENERAL INSTRUCTIONS AND DELIVERY/RETURN OPTIONS

1. Type or machine print all Public Records Filing forms, and submit with the correct FEE amount. (See FEE schedule on page 22.)

2. Choose a delivery/return option:

   a. **Regular mail** - If you are sending work in via regular mail, use the correct address:

   > New Jersey Department of the Treasury
   > Division of Revenue/Corporate Filing Unit
   > PO Box 308
   > Trenton, NJ 08625-0308

   All processed mail-in work will be returned via regular mail. Providing a self-addressed return envelope will speed processing. Otherwise, on a cover letter, indicate the return address if other than the registered office of the business entity.

   b. **Expedited/Over-the-Counter** - If you are expediting a filing (8.5 business hour processing), make sure that you deliver over-the-counter to: 225 W. State Street, 3rd Floor, Trenton, NJ 08608-1001, or have a courier/express mail service deliver to this address. Do not use USPS overnight delivery. Be sure to provide instructions as to how the filing is to be sent back to you: regular mail; front desk pick-up at 225 W. State Street; or delivery by courier/express mail. If you use a courier or express mail service for return delivery, be sure to provide a return package and completed air bill showing your name and company name (in the "to" and "from" blocks) and your courier account number.

   Notes: Use an acceptable payment method for mail and over-the-counter work:

   - Check or money order payable to the Treasurer, State of NJ;
   - Credit card -MASTERCARD/VISA or DISCOVER (provide card number, expiration date and name/address of card holder);
   - Depository account as assigned by the Treasurer; or
   - Cash.

   For over-the-counter **AND** mail-in submissions, remember to provide the required number of copies of the Public Record Filing. Filings for for-profit entities are submitted in duplicate and non-profit filings are done in triplicate.

   c. **Facsimile Filing Service (FFS)** - Transmit your filings to (609) 984-6851. You may request 8.5 business hour processing (EXPEDITED SERVICE), or same business day processing (SAME DAY SERVICE). Processing includes document review, fee accounting and acknowledgment turnaround.

   Payment Methods - You may pay for services via credit card (Master Card/Visa, Discover and American Express) or depository account (one payment method per request).

   Delivery/Turnaround - Barring difficulties beyond the Division of Revenue's control, including those that affect the Division of Revenue's data communication or data processing systems, all EXPEDITED requests delivered to the FFS workstation between 8:30 a.m. and 5:00 p.m. on workdays will be processed and returned within 8.5 business hours, while SAME DAY requests delivered by 12:00 noon on work days will be processed by 5:00 p.m. the same day. Requests received during off hours, weekends or holidays will be processed on the next work day, in 8.5 business hours. In the event of down time, upon system recovery, requests will be processed in receipt date/time order.

   Cover Sheet - with your transmission, send a cover sheet entitled
   > New Jersey Department of the Treasury
   > Division of Revenue
   > Facsimile Filing Service Request

   The cover sheet must include work request details: Name of firm or individual transmitting the service request; date of submission; depository account number or credit card number with expiration date; description of service requested e.g., "Certificate of Incorporation"; business name associated with the filing (proposed name for a new business entity); desired service level (EXPEDITED or SAME DAY); total number of pages in the request transmission, including cover sheet; and fax back number.

Note: The Division of Revenue will accept one filing per FFS. Requests lacking cover sheets or required cover sheet information may be rejected. Requests that do not contain a fax back number will not be processed. Also, if a service level is not specified, the Division of Revenue will assume that the request is for EXPEDITED service.

The Division of Revenue will make three attempts to transmit to the fax back number you provide. If the transmissions are unsuccessful, the Division of Revenue will send acknowledgments of completed filings to the registered office of the business entity involved via regular mail; or hold rejections in a pending file for two weeks, and dispose of the material thereafter.

Receiving Processed Work Back - For accepted work, the Division of Revenue will enter your Public Records Filing and Consolidated Registration application, and fax back an FFS Customer Transmittal with a copy of the approved Public Records Filing form stamped "FILED". For rejected work, the Division of Revenue will fax a FFS Customer Transmittal and Rejection Notice. If your submission is rejected, correct all defects and resubmit your filing as a new FFS request.

PAGE 23 INSTRUCTIONS

LINE BY LINE REQUIREMENTS FOR Public Records FILING

Item 1 **Business Name** - Enter a name followed by an acceptable designator indicating the type of business entity--for example: Inc., Corp., Corporation, Ltd., Co., or Company for a corporation; Limited Liability Company or L.L.C. for a Limited Liability Company; Limited Partnership or L.P. for a Limited Partnership; Limited Liability Partnership or L.L.P. for a Limited Liability Partnership.

> **Note:** The Division of Revenue will add an appropriate designator if none is provided.

Remember that the name must be distinguishable from other names on the State's data base. The Division of Revenue will check the proposed name for availability as part of the filing review process. If desired, you can reserve/register a name prior to submitting your filing by obtaining a reservation/registration. For information on name availability and reservation/registration services and fees, visit the Division's Web site at http://www.state.nj.us/njbgs/ or call (609) 292-9292 Monday - Friday, 8:30 a.m.- 4:30 p.m.

Item 2 **Type of Business Entity** - Enter the two or three letter code that corresponds with the type of business you are forming/registering:

Statutory Authority	Entity Type	Type Code
Title 14A	Domestic Profit	DP
For-Profit Corp.	Domestic Professional	PA
	Foreign Profit	FR
	(Incl. Foreign Professional Corp.)	
	Foreign Profit	DBA
	"Doing Business As"	
Title 15A	Domestic Non-Profit	NP
Non-Profit Corp.	Foreign Non-Profit	NF
Title 42:2B	Domestic LLC	LLC
Limited Liability Co.	Foreign LLC	FLC
Title 42:2A	Domestic LP	LP
Limited Partnership	Foreign LP	LF
Title 42	Domestic LLP	LLP
Limited Liability Partnership	Foreign LLP	FLP

N.J. INCORPORATING INSTRUCTIONS

Item 3 **Business Purpose** - Provide a brief description of the business purpose for the public record. If the business is a domestic for-profit corporation, you may leave this field blank and thereby rely on the general purpose clause provided in N.J.S.A. 14A: "The purpose for which this corporation is organized is(are) to engage in any activity within the purposes for which corporations may be organized under N.J.S.A. 14A:1-1 et seq."

Item 4 **Stock** - Domestic for-profit corporations only, list total shares.

Item 5 **Duration** - List the duration of the entity. If the duration is indefinite or perpetual, leave the field blank.

Item 6 **State of Formation/Incorporation**- Foreign entities only, list home state.

Item 7 **Date of Formation/Incorporation** - Foreign entities only, list the date of incorporation/formation in home state.

Item 8 **Contact Information** - Provide the following information:
a) **Registered Agent** - Enter one agent only. The agent may be an individual or a corporation duly registered, and in good standing with the State Treasurer.
b) **Registered Office** -Provide a New Jersey street address. A PO Box may be used only if the street address is listed as well.
c) **Main Business Address** - List the main or principal business street address in New Jersey.

Item 9 **Management** - For profit and professional corporations list initial Board of Directors, minimum of 1; domestic non-profits list Board of Trustees, minimum of 3; limited partnerships list all General Partners.

Item 10 **Incorporators** - Domestic profit, professional and non-profit corporations only, list incorporators, minimum of 1.

Signature Requirements for Public Records Filing:
The incorporator(s) and only the incorporator(s) may sign domestic profit, professional and non-profit corporate filings. Only the president, VP or Chief Executive Officer may sign foreign corporate filings. ALL general partners must sign limited partnership filings. ANY authorized representative may sign domestic or foreign limited liability company filings, while any authorized partner may sign domestic or foreign limited liability partnership filings.

PAGE 24 INSTRUCTIONS

Item 11   Provide additional "Entity-Specific" information as applicable.

Nonprofit corporations wanting Federal IRC section 501(c)(3) status are advised to consult the IRS concerning IRS required wording. The IRS telephone number is 1-877-829-5500, and the website is at www.irs.gov.

CHECKLIST FOR PUBLIC RECORDS FILING
- Completed and signed Public Records Filing (pages 23 and 24) *(Note: Use appropriate envelope supplied - P.O. Box 308)*
- Completed and signed Business Registration Application (pages 17-19) *(NOTE: Use appropriate envelope supplied-PO Box 252).*
- Filing fee using an acceptable payment method.
- Transmittal letter or service request sheet with instruction for returning completed work (mail and over-the-counter requests)
- Completed and signed CBT-2553 (S Corporation Election) if applicable
- Cover sheet listing work request details (FAX Filing Requests)

CHECKLIST FOR BUSINESS REGISTRATION APPLICATIONS
- Completed and signed Registration Application (pages 17-19)
- Completed and signed NJ-REG-L (Cigarette and Motor Fuel Wholesalers/Distributors/Manufacturers only) or CM-100 (Cigarette and Motor Fuel Retailers only, if applicable).

Delivery Options for:
Public Records Filings:
Mail: PO Box 308, Trenton, NJ 08625
Over-The-Counter: 225 W. State Street, 3rd Floor
                   Trenton, NJ 08608-1001
Phone: (609) 292-9292
FAX: (609) 984-6851

Business Registration Application:
Mail: PO Box 252, Trenton, NJ 08646-0252
Overnight: 847 Roebling Avenue, Trenton, NJ 08611
FAX: (609) 292-4291

FEE SCHEDULE
(Revised 7/1/02)

FAX FILING FEES (FFS)
- Each EXPEDITED FFS request is subject to a $15 fee, plus $1.00 per page fee for all accepted filings that are FAXED back for all Title 14A, Title 15A, and LP transactions.
  For LLCs and LLPs, each EXPEDITED FFS request is subject to a $25 fee, plus $1.00 per page fee for all accepted filings that are FAXED back.
- Each SAME DAY FFS request is subject to a $50 fee, plus a $1.00 per page fee, for all accepted filings that are FAXED back.
- These fees are in addition to the basic statutory fees associated with the filing itself.

BASIC FILING FEES
- Filing fee for all domestic entities, except non-profits, is $125 per filing; non-profit filing fee is $75 per filing.
- Filing fee for all foreign entities is $125 per filing.

SERVICE FEES AND OTHER OPTIONAL FEES (All added to basic filing fee, if selected.)
- Expediting Service Fee (8.5 business hours) is $15 per filing request for Title 14A, Title 15A and LP transactions.
- Expediting Service Fee (8.5 business hours) is $25 per filing request for LLCs and LLPs.
- Same Day Fee is $50 per filing request.
- Alternate Name Fee is $50 for each name.
- FAX Page Transmission Fee is $1.00 per page for all filings that are FAXED back.
- Certified Copies of Accepted Filings are $25 for each filed entity.

NOTE: THERE IS NO FILING FEE REQUIRED TO FILE FORM NJ-REG

N.J. INCORPORATING INSTRUCTIONS
(CONTINUED)

10
ASSISTANCE AVAILABLE TO HELP YOU GET STARTED

In recent years federal, state and local governments have begun to realize the importance of helping the small business owner. These various agencies have instituted and sponsored many programs to help the entrepreneur obtain money and learn about taxes. Almost all of the new assistance programs are without cost to the small business person. This section will concern itself with the government-sponsored groups, what they can do for you, and their locations in the State.

Your taxes are used to keep these groups active, so don't be afraid to seek out their help. All of the individuals involved in these programs have business experience and are interested in helping you make your business a success.

FEDERAL GOVERNMENT
SMALL BUSINESS ADMINISTRATION – S.B.A.

Every state has at least one S.B.A. district office staffed by a group of experts in financial, management and procurement assistance. These individuals are responsible for delivering S.B.A. programs to the state's small business community.

Some of these programs include direct and guaranteed loans to different groups. Borrowers in these programs may be small business concerns which cannot borrow from conventional lenders, minority or socially disadvantaged small business owners, and disaster victims.

The New Jersey District office is responsible for the delivery of SBA's many programs and services to 21 counties in NJ. Office hours are Monday - Friday 8:00 a.m. until 4:30 p.m.

SERVICES AVAILABLE:

1. Financial assistance through guaranteed loans made by area banks and lenders

2. Assistance to businesses owned by socially and economically disadvantaged individuals through 3(a) programs.

3. Free consulting through the network of Small Business Development Services

4. Free mentoring, advice, and information through SCORE - Counselors To America's Small Business

5. Women's Business Centers (WBCs) provide a wide range of servces to women entrepreneurs.

6. Business Information Centers (BICs) provide tools for new business or for existing businesses that need assistance in expanding or improving.

7. Special loan programs are available for businesses involved in international trade.

The S.B.A. office for the State of New Jersey is located at:

Two Gateway Center, 5th Floor, Suite 1501, Newark, New Jersey 07102
(973) 645-2434, fax 973-645-6265

INTERNAL REVENUE SERVICE ASSISTANCE

The I.R.S. also prints a number of publications dealing with various federal taxes. These materials can be obtained from local I.R.S. offices or on-line at www.irs.gov. Some of the guides that may be of interest to the small business person are:

NUMBER	TITLE
334	Tax Guide for Small Business
505	Tax Withholding and Estimated Tax
535	Business Expenses and Operating Loss
539	Withholding Taxes and Reporting Requirements
541	Tax Information on Partnerships
542	Tax Information on Corporations
552	Record Keeping Requirements
560	Tax Information on Self Employed
583	Record Keeping for a Small Business
587	Business Use of Your Home
589	Information on Sub Chapter S Corporations

Taxpayer assistance is available from the I.R.S. by calling the local office. The I.R.S. also holds several tax workshops during the year at offices around the State. You may contact any one of the following I.R.S. offices for more information.

Internal Revenue Service Locations in New Jersey
The Taxpayer Advocate Service: Call (973)921-4043 in Springfield or 1-877-777-4778 elsewhere. To make an appointment at an office call 844-545-5640

Atlantic County
5218 Atlantic Ave.
Mays Landing, NJ 08330
(609) 625-1376,

Bergen County
1Kalisa Way
Paramus, NJ 07652
(201) 634-7052

Camden County
57 Haddonfield Road
Cherry Hill, NJ 08002
(856) 321-1328

Essex County
20 Washington Place
Newark, NJ 07102
(973) 645-5543

Mercer County
One State St. Square
50 W. State Street
Trenton, NJ 08608
(609) 989-0533

Middlesex County
100 Dey Place, Wick Plaza
Edison, NJ 08817
(732) 572-9752

Monmouth County
4 Paragon Way.
Freehold, NJ 07728
(732) 660-0063

Morris County
Mt. Pleasant Office Bldg.
1719 Route 10 East
Parsippany, NJ 07054
(973) 808-0821

Passaic County
200 Federal Plaza
Paterson, NJ 07505
(973) 653-2676

Union County
200 Sheffield Street
Mountainside, NJ 07092
(908) 301-2112

SCORE Association

SCORE is a non-profit association dedicated to helping small businesses get off the ground, grow and achieve their goals through education and mentorship. Individuals who are already in business or who are planning on going into business can obtain FREE mentoring from SCORE. Supported by the Small Business Administration, SCORE is a network of volunteer business executives and professionals - mostly retired, but some still active - that provides small business with advice and mentoring. There is no charge for SCORE mentoring. For further information and/or assistance, contact the SCORE location nearest you or visit the web site at: *http://www.score.org/find-location.*

Locating chapters in New Jersey
Web site for New Jersey SCORE Chapters:
www.score.org/find-location?state=NJ

After you enter the web site address you will be taken to the page listing the current locaion in New Jersey. You have the option of calling a phone number, requesting a mentor, or obtaining directions. There is also a small window on the top right of the page which allows you to put in your zip code. That entry will take you to the nearest SCORE locaions closest to that zip code.

In addition to mentoring, SCORE also offers local workshops and webinars throughout the year at different locaions.

SCORE provides:
• Volunteer mentors who share their expertise across 62 industries
• Free, confidential business mentoring in person, via email or by video
• Free business tools, templates and tips online
• Inexpensive or free workshops (locally) and webinars (online 24/7)

SCORE is headquartered at 1175 Herndon Parkway, suite 900, Herndon, Virginia 20170. Their phone number is 1-800-634-0245. Technical support - help@score.org.

STATE PROGRAMS
Small Business Assistance Office

The Office of Small Business Assistance was recently established with the New Jersey Department of Commerce and Economic Development. Some of the functions of this office are:

1. Establishment of a loan referral program for small business

2. Keep in close contact with the Department of the Treasury to promote contracts with small business firms

3. Receive complaints from small businesses

4. Study laws affecting small businesses

For assistance contact:

> Office of Small Business Assistance
> New Jersey Department of Commerce &
> Growth Commission
> Mary Roebling Bldg.
> 20 W. State St., CN 835
> Trenton, New Jersey 08625
> (609) 984-4442

The office of Promoting Technical Innovation is located in the New Jersey Department of Commerce and Growth Commission. The office was established to stimulate and encourage the development of new commercial products to be manufactured in New Jersey. The services provided include: communication among inventors, sources of capital, technical consultations, information on available research and development grants, and assistance in the preparation of applications.

For assistance contact:

> Office of Promoting Technical Innovation
> New Jersey Department of Commerce & Growth Commission
> Trenton, New Jersey 08625   (609) 292-7138

Small Business Development Centers

Small Business Development Centers (SBDC) are state-operated programs, funded jointly by the U.S. Small Business Administration (SBA) and the State government hosting the program. These centers serve as an umbrella under which resources are collected for the exclusive use of small business owners and future entrepreneurs.

The centers provide one-on-one counseling and training in management and financial planning through public and private sources, trade and business associations, and students and faculty associated with universities or colleges in which S.B.D.C.'s are generally located. Website www.njsbdc.com

NJSBDC HEADQUARTERS
Rtugers Business School
Brenda B. Hopper, State Director
1 Washington Park, Suite 360
Newark, NJ 07102
(973) 353-1927 • FAX: (973) 353-1110
e-mail: bhopper@njsbdc.com

ATLANTIC/CAPEMAY/CUMBERLAND COUNTIES
Carol Waties, Director
Stockton University
35 Martin Luther King Blvd.
Atlantic City, NJ 08401
(609) 626-3889

BERGEN COUNTY COMMUNITY COLLEGE
Ramapo College of NJ
Anisfield School of Business
Vincent Vicari, Director
505 Ramapo Valley Road
Mahwah, NJ 07430
(201) 684-7135

MONMOUTH/OCEAN
Brookdale Community College
Jackeline Fuertes, Director
ATEC Building, room 111
765 Newman Springs Road
Lincroft, NJ 07738
www.mosbdc.com
(732) 842-8685 • FAX: (732) 842-0203
(732) 255-0468 - Ocean Office

KEAN UNIVERSITY
David Margulies, Director
Willis Hall, 1000 Morris Avenue
Union, NJ 07083
(908) 737-4220 • FAX: (980) 527-2960

MERCER/MIDDLESEX
Lorraine Allen, Director
2000 Pennington Avenue
Forcina Hall 253
Ewing, NJ 08628
(609) 771-2947

NEW JERSEY CITY UNIVERSITY
Barbara S. O'Neal, Director
285 Westside Ave, Suite 189-191
Jersey City, NJ 07305
(201) 200-2156 • FAX: (201) 200-3404

RARITAN VALLEY COMMUNITY COLLEGE
Bill Harnden, Director
14 Vogt Drive
Bridgewater, NJ 08807
(908) 526-1200 Ext. 8515
FAX: (908) 725-9687

RUTGERS UNIVERSITY - NEWARK CAMPUS
Tandai Ndoro, PhD, Regional Director
25 James Street
Newark, NJ 07102
(973) 353-5950 • FAX: (973) 353-5970

RUTGERS UNIVERSITY - NEW BRUNSWICK
Elayne McClain, Regional Director
100 Rockafeller Road Ste 4005C
Piscataway, NJ 08854
(848) 445-8790

RUTGERS UNIVERSITY - CAMDEN CAMPUS
Bob Palumbo, Director
419 Cooper Street
Camden, NJ 08102
Website: http://www.rsbdc.org
(856) 225-6221 • FAX: (856) 225-6621

WARREN COUNTY
Dolores Stammer, Director
150 Mountain Avenue
Mountain Business Center, Suite 2-4
Hackettstown, NJ 07840
(908) 269-8475

WILLIAM PATERSON UNIVERSITY
Kate Muldoon, Director
131 Ellison Street
Paterson, NJ 07505
(973) 973-321-1378

NJSBDC SPECIALTY PROGRAMS Procurement - Shy Hopkins   E-Business
International Trade - Roger Cohen (973) 353-1927   (973) 353-1352

US Dept of Commerce - http://export.gov/

LOCAL & STATEWIDE ASSISTANCE

Many people who start their own business don't know who to contact for information on local licenses, permits, and occupancy information. The most helpful group in your area would be the Chamber of Commerce. These groups are organized specifically to assist businesses wanting to start a venture in the chamber's area of location. The various Chambers of Commerce throughout the state are listed on the following pages.

Another organization is the S.B.A. Certified Development Companies presently located in counties throughout the state. Certified Development Companies (CDCs) are nonprofit corporations certified and regulated by the SBA, that work with participating lenders to provide financing to small businesses. There are 270 CDCs nationwide, each covering a specific geographic area.

CERTIFIED DEVELOPMENT COMPANIES

UCEDC, a nonprofit economic development corporation
75 Chestnut Street
Cranford, NJ 07016
Phone: 908-527-1166
Fax: 908-527-1207

Across Nations Pioneers, Inc.
15 Eagle Streetm, Suite 107
Englewood, NJ 07631
Phone: 201-541-4101
Fax: 201-541-4130

New Jersey Business Finance Corporation
2050 Centr Avenue, Suite 375
Fort Lee, NJ 07024
Phone: 201-346-0300
Fax: 201-346-1336

Trenton Business Assistance Corporation
3111 Quakerbridge Road, 2nd Floor
Mercerville, NJ 08619
Phone: 609-587-1133
Fax: 609-587-1313

Four County Development, Inc.
161 Main Road
Montville, NJ 07005

CHAMBERS OF COMMERCE IN NEW JERSEY

New Jersey State Chamber of Commerce: (609) 989-7888
216 West State Street, Trenton, NJ 08608 Fax: (609) 989-9696
Statewide Hispanic Chamber of Commerce of NJ: (201) 451-9512
One Gateway Center, Suite 2409, Newark, NJ 07102
www.shccnj.org

North Jersey Regional Chamber of Commerce: (973) 470-9300
1033 Route 46 East, Suite A103, Clifton, NJ 07013

Aberdeen: (see Matawan)
Asbury Park: P.O. Box 649, 07712, (732) 775-7676
Atlantic City: 1125 Atlantic Ave., 08401, (609) 345-5600
Avalon: 30th & Ocean Dr., 08202, (609) 967-3936
Bamber Lake: (see Forked River)
Bay Head: (see Point Pleasant)
Bayonne: 621 Ave. C, P.O. Box 266, 07002, (201) 436-4333
Belleville: PO Box 284, 07109, (973) 759-4848
Belmar: 1005^1/2 Main St., P.O. Box 297, 07719, (732) 681-2900
Bergenfield: 35 Washington Ave., 07621, (201) 387-8300
Berkeley Heights: (see Summit)
Bloomfield: 277 Broad St., 07003, (973) 748-2000
Bloomingdale: P.O. Box 100, 07403, (973) 838-1104
Boonton: P.O. Box 496, 07005, (973) 334-4117
Bogota: 60 W. Main, PO Box 215, 07603
Bordentown: 11 Walnut St., P.O. Box 65, 08505, (609) 298-7774
Bound Brook: P.O. Box 227, 08805, (732) 356-7273
Brick: 270 Chambers Bridge Rd., 08723, (732) 477-4949
Bridgeton: 53 S. Laurel St., P.O. Box 1063, 08302, (609) 455-1312
Brigantine: P.O. Box 484, 08203, (609) 266-3437
Budd Lake: 98 Route 46, Village Green Annex, P.O. Box 192, 07828,
(973) 691-0109
Burlington: P.O. Box 67, 08016, (609) 387-0963
Burlington County: (see Mt. Laurel)
Butler: (see Bloomingdale)
Caldwell: (see W. Caldwell)
Cape May: 513 Washington St. Mall - 2nd Floor, P.O. Box 556, 08204,
(609) 884-5508
Cape May Court House: PO Box 6, 08210, (609) 463-1655
Cedar Grove: (see West Caldwell)
Carney's Point: 91A S. Virginia Ave., 08069, (856) 299-6699
Chatham: P.O. Box 231, 07928, (973) 635-2444
Cherry Hill: 1060 N. Kings Hwy., 08034 (856) 667-1600
Clifton: P.O. Box 110, 07011, (973) 470-9300

Colts Neck: (see Greater Monmouth)
Cranford: 8 Springfield Ave., P.O. Box 165, 07016, (908) 272-6114
Dennis Township: (see Ocean View)
Denville: P.O. Box 333, 07834 (973) 627-1340
East Brunswick: P.O. Box 56, 08816, (732) 257-3009
Eastern Monmouth: 170 Broad St.,Red Bank 07701, (732) 741-0055
East Orange: P.O. Box 731, 07019, (973) 674-0900
Eatontown: (see Red Bank)
Edison: 100 Menlo Park #209, 08817, (732) 494-0300
Egg Harbor City: P.O. Box 129, 08215, (609) 965-0260
Elizabeth:135 Jefferson Ave., P.O. Box 300, 07207-0300, (908)352-0900
Elmwood Park: 511 Boulevard, 07407, (201) 797-5008
Englewood: 2-10 N. Van Brunt St., 07631, (201) 567-2381
Englewood Cliffs: P.O. Box 954, 07632, (201) 567-9344
Fair Lawn: 0-100 27th St., 07410, (201) 796-7050
Fairview: 202 Anderson Ave., 07022, (201) 945-3707
Farmingdale: P.O. Box 534, 07727, (732) 919-0149
Forked River: 103 Route 9 N., P.O. Box 306, 08731, (609) 693-8312
Fort Lee: 210 Whitman St., 07024, (201) 944-7575
Franklin Lakes: P.O. Box 149, 07417, (201) 891-7609
Franklin Township: 1717 Amwell Rd, Somerset, 08873, (732) 873-1717
Freehold: (see Greater Monmouth)
Garfield: P.O. Box 525, 07026, (973) 773-7500
Glassboro: PO Box 651, 08028, (609) 881-7900
Glen Rock: P.O. Box 176, 07452, (201) 447-3434
Greater Monmouth: 18 Schanck Rd.Suite C3, Freehold Twsp., 07728
     (732) 462-3030
Hackensack: 302 Union St., 07601, (201) 489-3700
Hackettstown: P.O. Box 546, 07840, (908) 852-1253
Hammonton: 10 S. Egg Harbor Rd., P.O. Box 554, 08037, (609) 561-9080
Hasbrouck Heights: PO Box 1, 07604, (201) 599-5822
Hawthorne: 471 Lafayette Ave., P.O. Box 331, 07507, (973) 427-5078
Hightstown: P.O. Box 87, 08520, (609) 448-4412
Hillside: PO Box 965, 07205, (908) 946-5130
Howell: P.O. Box 196, 07731, (732) 363-4114
Irvington: P.O. Box 323, 07111, (973) 372-4100
Jersey City: 253 Washington St., 07302, (201) 435-7400
Kearney: 764 Kearney Ave., 07032, (201) 991-5600
Keyport: PO Box 785, 07735, (732) 264-3626
Lake Hopatcong: P.O. Box 64, 07849 (973) 361-2810
Lakewood: 395 Hwy 70 #125, 08701, (732) 363-0012
Lambertville: 239 N. Union St., 08530, (609) 397-0055
Lanoka Harbor: (see Forked River)

Lebanon: 2200 Route 31, Suite 15, 08833, (908) 735-5955
Ledgewood: P.O. Box 436, 07852, (973) 770-0740
Livingston: 154 S. Livingston Ave., 07039, (973) 992-4343
Lodi: P.O. Box 604, 07644, (973) 777-9687
Long Branch: 628 Broadway, 07740, (732) 222-0400
Madison: P.O. Box 152, 07940, (973) 377-7830
Mahwah: P.O. Box 506, 07430
Manahawkin: (see Ship Bottom)
Manasquan: P.O. Box 365, 08736, (732) 223-8303
Maplewood, PO Box 423, 07040 (201) 761-4333
Marlboro: (see Greater Monmouth)
Matawan: P.O. Box 522, 07747, (732) 290-1125
Maywood: 140 W. Pleasant Ave., 07607, (201) 843-3111
Metuchen: 323 Main St., 08840, (732) 548-2964
Middletown: Union Square Mall, P.O. Box 424, 07748, (732) 671-3360
Midland Park: P.O. Box 267, 07432, (973) 423-5815
Millburn: P.O. Box 651, 07041, (973) 379-1198
Millville: 100 N. High St., P.O. Box 831, 08332 (856) 825-2600
Montclair: 26 Parks St., #2025, 07042, (973) 744-7660
Montville: 195 Change Bridge Rd., 07045, (973) 263-3310
Morristown: 25 Lindsley Dr., 07960, (973) 539-3882
Mount Freedom: PO Box 391, 07970, (973) 361-3462
New Brunswick: 1091 Aaron Rd., North Brunswick, 08902, (732)821-1700
New Brunswick: 123 Church St., 08901, (732) 545-4800
New Providence: (see Summit)
Newark: 744 Broad St, 26th Floor, 07102, (973) 242-4209
Newton: 120 Hampton House Rd., 07860, (973) 579-1811,
North Caldwell: (see West Caldwell)
Northern Monmouth: 500 Hwy 36, Navesink 07752, (732) 291-7870
Nutley: 610 Franklin Ave., 07110, (973) 667-5300
Oakland: P.O. Box 8, 07436, (201) 337-7117
Ocean City: P.O. Box 157, 08226, (609) 399-1412
Ocean County: (see Toms River)
Ocean Grove: P.O. Box 415, 07756, (732) 774-1391
Oceanview: PO Box 85, 08230, (609) 624-2276
Old Bridge: P.O. Box 5241, 08857, (732) 607-6340
Orange: POBox 1178, 07050, (973) 676-8725
Paramus: P.O. Box 325, 07652, (201) 261-3344
Parsippany: 959 Rte. 46 #101, 07054, (201) 402-6400
Passaic: (see Clifton)
Paterson: 100 Hamilton Plaza, 07505, (973) 881-7300
Perth Amboy: 214 Smith St., 08862, (973) 442-7400
Phillipsburg: 675 Corliss Ave., 08865, (908) 859-5161
Piscataway: 1 Possumtown Rd., 08854, (732) 394-0220
Plainfield: 120 W. 7th St., 07060, (908) 754-7250

Point Pleasant: 517 A. Arnold Ave., 08742, (732) 899-2424
Pompton Lakes: PO Box 129, 07442, (973) 839-0187
Princeton: Princeton Forrestal Village, 216 Rockingham Row, 08540,
    (609) 520-1776
Rahway: P.O. Box 595-C, 07065, (732) 429-0555
Randolph: (see Mount Freedom)
Raritan: P.O. Box 236, 08869, (908) 429-0555
Ridgewood: 199 Dayton St., 07450, (201) 445-2600
Ringwood, 109 Skyline Dr., P.O. Box 62, 07456, (973) 835-7998
Roxbury: (see Ledgewood)
Rutherford: P.O. Box 216, 07070, (201) 933-5230
Saddlebrook: 50 Market St. 07663, (201) 556-0123
Salem: (see Carney's Point)
Sayreville: (see Old Bridge)
Short Hills: (see Millburn)
Somerset: 15 Cedar Grove Ln. #9-A, 08873, (973) 560-3737
Somerville: P.O. Box 833, 08876, (732) 725-1552
South Amboy: (see Old Bridge)
Southern Monmouth: P.O. Box 1305, Wall 07719, (732) 974-1151
Southern Ocean: 265 W. 9th St., Ship Bottom 08008, (609) 494-7211
South Orange: P.O. Box 621, 07079, (973) 762-4333
Sparta: P.O. Box 444, 07871, (973) 729-7700
Stone Harbor: PO Box 422, 08247, (609) 368-6101
Summit: P.O. Box 824, 07902, (908) 522-1700
Sussex County: (see Newton)
Tenafly: 78 County Rd., P.O. Box 163, 07670, (201) 894-0568
Toms River: 1200 Hooper Ave., 08753, (732) 349-0220
Towaco: (see Clifton)
Trenton: 214 W. State St., 08608, (609) 393-4143
Union: 355 Chestnut St., 07083, (908) 688-2777
Vernon: PO Box 308, 07462, (973) 764-0764
Vineland: P.O. Box 489, 08360-0489, (856) 691-7400
Voorhees: Piazza 6014 at Main St., 08043, (856) 424-7776
Wayne: 2055 Hamburg Turnpike, 07470, (973) 831-7788
West Caldwell: 3 Fairfield Ave., 07006, (973) 226-5500
West Hudson: (see Kearny)
West Milford: P.O. Box 234, 07480, (973) 728-3150
West New York: 428 60th St., P.O. Box 1145, 07093, (201) 295-5065
Westfield: P.O. Box 81, 07090, (908) 233-3021
Westwood: P.O. Box 155, 07675, (201) 664-8468
Wildwood: 3601 Boardwalk, 08260, (609) 729-4000
Woodbridge: 52 Main St., 07095, (732) 636-4040
Woodbury: Kings Hwy., P.O. Box 363, 08096, (856) 845-4056
Wyckoff: P.O. Box 2, 07481, (201) 891-3616

New Jersey Business Owners Associations

NJ BUSINESS & INDUSTRY ASSOCIATION
10 W. Lafayette Street, Trenton, NJ 08608   (609) 393-7707

NATIONAL ASSOCIATION OF WOMEN BUSINESS OWNERS (NAWBO)
1-800-556-2926, www.nawbo.org
Central Jersey Chapter, www.nawbocentraljersey.org
South Jersey Chapter, www.nawbosouthjersey.org

NJ ASSOCIATION OF WOMEN BUSINESS OWNERS, INC. (NJAWBO)
549 Pompton Ave, Suite 107
Cedar Grove, NJ 07009
(609) 308-2530, njawbo@njawbo.org

NEW JERSEY TECHNOLOGY COUNCIL
1001 Briggs Rd, Suite 280, Mt. Laurel, NJ 08054
(856) 787-9700

Helpful Links for Starting a Business in New Jersey

Small Business Administration   http://www.sba.gov/

Small Business Development Centers   http://www.njsbdc.com

SCORE   http://www.score.org/

State of New Jersey Department of Treasury
                    http://www.state.nj.us/treasury/taxation

Internal Revenue Service   http://www.irs.gov

Entrepreneurs (beginning business owners) http://www.entrepreneur.com

NJ Chambers of Commerce and Business Associations
                    http://www.2chambers.com/new6.htm

11
SELECTING AN ACCOUNTANT

Many people have approached me and asked the question – "How do you select an accountant?" Then when you do pick one, how do you know if he/she is really doing for you what you need? Here is an approach to help start your search for an accountant:

1. **Seek out someone who owns a business similar to yours.**

2. **Be sure that the size of the establishment and annual sales are on a par with your new business expectations.**

3. **Ask the owner to give you the name of his accountant.**

4. **Give the accountant a call, explain your situation and request an appointment.**

I have discovered that many new business owners decide to start their own venture without the advice or assistance of a professional. Some business owners will invest thousands of dollars, incorporate and sign long-term contracts without having contacted an accountant or attorney.

You should be sure to enlist the help of a professional accountant prior to starting your new business. The beginning fees will not be significant, but the advice you obtain will be immeasurable. This professional will help you select the proper type of enterprise, set up your books, apply for identification numbers, and prepare your tax forms.

Another source might be an accounting or business management instructor at a college. More than likely these individuals will have part-time accounting practices with a number of smaller clients. Approach any one of the instructors and inquire of their expertise in the area of your new venture. Ask if they have other clients in the same business. Then inquire if you can spend some time with them to discuss your new business.

There are also many seminars given during the year that are sponsored by the S.B.A., S.C.O.R.E., Chambers of Commerce, Small Business Development Center, Community Colleges, and the New Jersey Office of Small Business. I suggest that you attend a few of these meetings for the information and literature that is distributed. Almost always there is an accountant present, giving a talk on the successful operation of a small business. This individual is one that you might want to seek out for professional advice in running your new business. Approach him/her to see if they could spend some time with you to review your business proposal.

More than likely the accountants will charge you some minimal fee for the time spent in their office. Don't waste their time, get to the point and present your case.

During the interview with the prospective accountant, pose the following questions, preferably in this order:

1. Have you ever taken care of my type of business?

2. How often will you come to work on my account?

3. What will you do for me?

4. How often will you bill me?

5. How much will you charge for the work to be performed?

Presently, the fee for most accountants who charge by the hour is $150 to $275 per hour. The average is about $200 per hour.

Here is what your accountant should do for you.

Always should be able to:

- **Prepare corporate or partnership tax forms**
- **Handle all I.R.S. audits**
- **Handle all New Jersey audits**
- **Prepare financial statements**
- **Prepare your personal tax form 1040**
- **Go to your bank with you when needed for a loan**

If not completed by you or your bookkeeper, your accountant should be able to:

- Prepare Federal and State Payroll reports

- Prepare New Jersey business personal property tax forms

- Prepare New Jersey sales tax forms

- Prepare New Jersey gross income tax monthly forms

- Prepare monthly depository cards – FICA, Federal Withholding Tax

- Do checkbook bank reconciliation
- Write up a cash receipts and disbursements journal
- Set up and post to a general ledger

Remember, no matter who you select as an accountant, be sure you are comfortable with this person. Don't pick someone just because your relative used them and their prices are low. They must instill some professional confidence in you and respect you as a client. Their advice is invaluable so make use of it, ask questions, and make sure you get what you pay for.

12
CONCLUSION

Now that you have read this manual, you should feel more confident to take that big step into the world of business ownership.

Being your own boss is great . . . when it works. Be sure to ask questions and seek professional assistance as soon as you feel the need for help.

The proper use of accounting and legal advice throughout your business career will hopefully prevent those major catastrophes that befall many new owners.

This manual has provided you with an introduction into the business environment. Take the time to acquire as much knowledge about your new business as possible. Subscribe to business magazines and read some of the small business texts that are available in your local library.